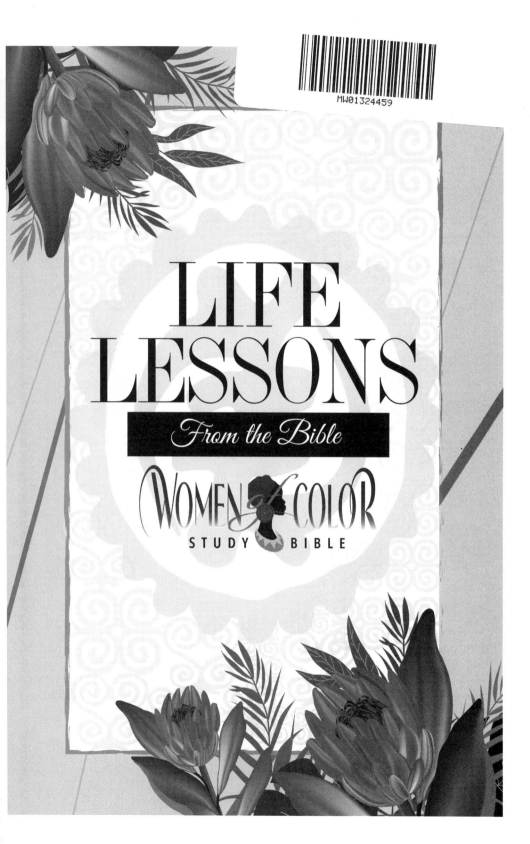

© 2020 BY URBAN SPIRIT, LLC. ALL RIGHTS RESERVED No part of this document may be reproduced or transmitted in any form or by any means, electronic, mechanical, photocopying, or otherwise without prior written permission of Urban Spirit, LLC. All scripture quotations, unless otherwise indicated, are taken from the King James Version Bible.

Production: Livingstone LLC.
Cover and interior designed by Larry P. Taylor

OLD TESTAMENT LIFE LESSONS

From the Bible

GENESIS LIFE LESSONS

GENESIS 1-2

Chapters one and two record the creation of the universe, including the solar system, plants, fowl and other animals, and humankind. Fundamental to successful living in this world is the affirmation that the universe is not accidental, but the handiwork of an all-wise and all-powerful God. While we may not have all the details of how all things came into existence, we can confirm who created them.

> *Creating Wonder, I acknowledge and praise You for bringing all things into existence, including me. Help me to worship and appreciate You through the beauty of our world. Create in me a hunger to join You in the continuing creation left in our hands!*

GENESIS 3

Chapter three relates the story of Adam and Eve's disobedience to God's Law, and their consequent expulsion from the Garden of Eden. It is because of Adam and Eve's alienation from God that each successive generation would be required to seek salvation through Jesus, who was God in human form, sent to earth as a man to redeem us.

Ancient of Days, I acknowledge that I, too, am a sinner, and fall short of Your glory. I thank You for knowing me and accepting me as I am. Help me to accept the grace of your forgiveness when I ask You for it because of the atoning sacrifice of Jesus, Your Son.

GENESIS 11—12

Chapters 11 and 12 tell us that in order to separate the children of Israel from other nations, God called upon Abram and Sarai (later renamed by God as Abraham and Sarah) to establish a nation, one that would ultimately produce the Savior. They are required to leave their homeland, Ur, and settle in Canaan. It was this journey of faith that symbolized the restoration of God's faith in man through the person of Abram (Abraham).

Dear God, help me, like Abram and Sarai, to obey Your clearly revealed will. When I am unsure of Your will, help me to trust You to clarify the path I should take.

GENESIS 15–17

In Genesis 15 and 17, God establishes two covenants with Abraham: The first was a promise to give Abraham and his descendants the land of Canaan; the second was the promise of a child born to Sarah that would signify the beginning of the Hebrew nation.

Covenant-Maker, help me to identify in Your Living Word those promises You have made for my benefit. Then, help me to trust You to fulfill them.

EXODUS LIFE LESSONS

EXODUS 1

Shiphrah and Puah, Hebrew midwives, feared God and did not kill Hebrew children, thereby disobeying the Egyptian pharaoh. With passive resistance and covert actions, these two women defied the wicked law of Pharaoh. With great risk to their own lives, these women contradicted man-made laws to work with the God of Israel. "We must obey God before humans" (Acts 4:19). Like them, and the more recent examples of Ms. Rosa Parks and Dr. Martin Luther King, Jr., we must be prepared to suffer for our convictions.

Birthing God, You who give birth to thoughts, dreams, and visions, help me to be ready to participate with You in bringing forth renewed life.

EXODUS 2

Moses had a passionate desire to see his people liberated from Egyptian bondage—not unlike other leaders who see their people enslaved. Moses lashed out, killing one Egyptian at a time—a method that was doomed. As events unfold in the Book of Exodus, we can see that God never chided Moses for desiring liberation. Rather, God directed him to use a more effective strategy—the divine strategy. The human desire for liberation is undeniable. Such efforts must be God-directed and God-empowered to be effective.

> *Liberator,* give me a heart for freedom! Loose the shackles from my mind in order that I may be free to live fully for You.

EXODUS 3

"I have surely seen the afflictions of my people which are in Egypt, and have heard their cry by reason of their taskmasters; for I know their sorrows; And I am come down to deliver them out of the hand of the Egyptians" (Ex. 3:7–8) reveals God's perfect knowledge and passionate concern for Israel. Though God may not respond when we think God should and in the ways we think, God cares and will respond at the right time and in the best way. Until the Ancient of Days acts, we must trust, wait, and be of good courage (Psalm 27:14).

> *Seeing,* Hearing, Knowing, and Coming One, I stand in awe of Your awareness of my every need.

"I AM THAT I AM" (Ex. 3:14). God revealed Himself to Moses as the "I AM." In doing so, God conveyed to Moses that the pre-existing, self-sustaining One needed no external help. God's words to Moses assured him that Yahweh was totally capable of being whatever Israelites—or anyone—would need!

> *Great I AM, thank You for being present with me even now. Help me to remember that You are not known as the Great used to be!*

EXODUS 4

Moses offered several excuses to avoid accepting God's commission (Ex. 4:1, 13), but in the end he obeyed (Ex. 4:19–20). God never objects to our honesty in questioning the direction for our lives. Nevertheless, to disobey is not wise, as many servants of God have discovered.

> *Perfect Direction, thank You for providing perfect guidance in my life. Thank You for an example in the women who steadfastly held to their commissions. Enable me to follow them in faithfulness.*

EXODUS 7–11

Ten plagues were inflicted upon Pharaoh and the Egyptians before the Israelites were finally released after 430 years of servitude. One cannot fathom God's timing in bringing deliverance. Those who insist that God must always answer their prayers at the time and in the manner they prescribe have a lot to learn about God. This chapter provides us with the laments of distraught mothers who arose, early in the morning, to discover their oldest sons were dead. There was no comfort for their grief.

> ***Prayer-Answering God,** thank You for our freedom and deliverance, regardless of the various attempts to keep us enslaved.*

EXODUS 12

Applying blood to the doorposts and eating the Passover lamb were prerequisites for experiencing deliverance from the angel of death and Egyptian bondage. The blood symbolized the people's trust in the provision God made to spare their firstborn—the slain lamb died that their children might live. Eating the meat symbolized the Israelites' acceptance of God's provision. That symbolism would eventually apply to the Lord Jesus who became God's Lamb to take away the sins of the world (John 1:29). Our trust in the atoning sacrificial death of Jesus Christ on the cross brings deliverance from the bondage of sin and birth into His eternal kingdom.

> ***Passover Lamb,** how amazing is Your self-giving blood sacrifice that allows me to bypass death and destruction and grants me eternal life!*

"A mixed multitude went up also with them" (Ex. 12:38). This mixed group undoubtedly consisted of non-Hebrews who decided to cast their lot with the Israelites and their God. As such, the group, which eventually arrived in Canaan, was mixed—held together by the Sinaitic covenant under the leadership of Moses and, later, Joshua. God's true church today is a "mixed" group of people, all of whom declare Jesus Christ to be Lord.

> *Calling God, I'm grateful that You allow the mixed-up, messed-up, and confused to be included among those You call Your people.*

EXODUS 13

"God led the people about through the way of the wilderness" (Ex. 13:18). The distance between Egypt and Canaan was less than 200 miles. The Israelites could have made the journey in a few days if they had taken the shortest route, but God had other plans. Because God knew what lay ahead—and the disobedient mindset of the people—the 40-year period of wandering was a learning experience. Similarly, sometimes we are led in round-about ways because God knows things we do not. We can accept God's way for us as best even when we do not understand it (Ps. 32:8).

> *Leading God, Your way is always perfect, even when I'm feeling as if I'm in charge. Lead me, guide me, along life's way. With You in charge, I cannot stray.*

EXODUS 14

"And Moses said unto the people, Fear ye not, stand still, and see the salvation of the Lord ... The Lord shall fight for you, and ye shall hold your peace" (14:13–14). At certain times in our Christian walk, we must "stand still, and see the salvation of the Lord." At other times we must—in faith—get moving! Knowing when to act is critical. Through faith and fellowship with God, and in a covenant relationship with other like-minded Christians, we discover the appropriate action at the right moment.

> ***Direction Provider,*** *make Your will for my life clear. Strengthen me to know the difference between Your will and mine, and then, to follow Your directions.*

The dance of the prophet Miriam and all the women is recorded after the triumphal crossing over the Red Sea from slavery into freedom. "For the horse of Pharaoh went in with his chariots and with his horsemen into the sea, and the Lord brought again the waters of the sea upon them; but the children of Israel went on dry land in the midst of the sea. And Miriam the prophet, the sister of Aaron, took a timbrel in her hand; and all the women went out after her with timbrels and with dances. .And Miriam answered them, Sing ye to the Lord, for he hath triumphed gloriously; the horse and his rider hath he thrown into the sea" (Ex. 15:19–21). Miriam led in celebration with authority that called all the other women to follow. The song of praise she sang is recorded. She wrote liturgy and performed liturgical dance without question or censor. What happened later to end her leadership role is not clear. There is no further transmission of her title or function. However, we do know that she was used by God to lead in worship and praise.

> ***Lord of the Dance,*** *when the horse and riders in my life have been drowned by Your greatness, teach me, like Miriam, to dance and to sing for the victory!*

EXODUS 17

"Is the Lord among us, or not?" (Ex. 17:7). The people were thirsty and complained to Moses. God instructed Moses to strike a rock with the shepherd's rod he had used to bring down calamity upon the Egyptians. The place was called Massah to memorialize the people's testing of God, and Meribah to memorialize their arguing with God. Despite all God had done in delivering the people and providing food and meat, they complained and questioned God's commitment to provide for them. Though we are invited to come boldly and lay our every petition before God, we grieve the compassionate heart of God when we, like the Israelites, question God's love for and commitment to us.

> ***Omnipresent Wonder,*** *forgive me for "forgetting" that You are committed to my highest good, trustworthy without a doubt, and faithful to Your every promise.*

EXODUS 18

Moses' father-in-law visits him and notices how he attempted to do all the work himself. Jethro counsels him to share the load with others. The principle of dividing and sharing authority and responsibilities is one that has enabled giant corporations and governments to accomplish much more than they would otherwise have. Still, some leaders try to do everything, only to burn themselves out.

> *Almighty Counselor, gift me with administrative insight, so that the ministry You have called me to fulfill might not become a burden.*

EXODUS 19–24

The Israelites agree to a covenant that Yahweh will be their God and they will obey Him willingly (Ex. 24:3). The covenant (Ex. 20) follows the pattern of ancient covenants: God identifies Himself as the God who delivers them and then establishes expectations of them. While the Sinaitic covenant was a specific agreement between God (Yahweh) and the Israelites, the Ten Commandments reflect His eternal moral foundation applicable at all times to all people. The New Testament makes clear we are not justified by keeping the Law (Gal. 3:11); however, the same New Testament makes clear we must not violate the principles of these commandments (Matt. 5:17–20; James 2:10–11).

Covenant-Making and Covenant-Keeping
God, enable me to keep my word. Thank You for keeping covenant with me, even when I've failed.

EXODUS 25–30

The tabernacle, with all its furnishings, reflected the Egyptian influence in design. While God gave clear instructions on what these items of worship were to look like, this apparently did not rule out the use of furniture-building knowledge. More important is that God provided a means whereby the Israelites could approach a holy God. Similarly, God has provided Jesus Christ as our High Priest so we can approach the throne to find gracious help in our times of need (Heb. 4:14–16).

Divine Designer, build my life to be pleasing for dwelling in Your presence.

EXODUS 32

While Moses was upon Mount Sinai receiving the Ten Commandments, Israel turned to idolatry and revelry. God threatened to destroy them. Moses interceded on behalf of the people, and God retreated. How much divine anger has been turned away because some saintly father or mother poured out his or her heart to God on behalf of a wayward child? Praise God for intercessors!

Faithful God, thank You for the magnificent gift of Your amazing grace. I continue to turn to forms of idolatry and even revelry, despite my very best intentions. Yet, You continue to intercede on my behalf. Be glorified through my life.

LEVITICUS LIFE LESSONS

LEVITICUS 1–6

In order to draw near to God and remain in harmony with God, two major categories of sacrifice were employed—joyful and sorrowful—both of which consisted of purification and guilt sacrifices. Many complex details were involved with these demanding, bloody rituals. Many occasions, seasons, and festivals required the fulfilling of vows before the priest. The word sacrifice in Hebrew means "to draw near," and in English is more clearly rendered as "to make sacred." The offerings were to be a means of compensation for sins and protection from divine punishment. The underlying purpose of sacrifice was to keep the people in harmony with their God. A handbook, Leviticus, was required to ensure an orderly and decent method of being right with God.

Lord, prepare me to be a sacrifice acceptable in Your sight.

LEVITICUS 7–8

The trespass, peace, thanksgiving, free will, and vow offerings are outlined in this section of Leviticus. It was the responsibility of the women in Levite households to ensure the purity of their house through the keeping of a kosher kitchen and diet. Unmarried females were allowed to eat from the holy sacrifices. However, no woman was allowed to eat from the most holy sacrifices, which were the burnt guilt and sin offerings; these were restricted to the male priests. In the days of the temple, Levite women sang, played musical instruments, participated in choirs, and choreographed and performed sacred dances based on the dances led by the prophet Miriam. Home rituals were oftentimes left in the hands of capable and trusted women.

> ***Holy One,*** *purify me so that I might serve You in all I do.*

LEVITICUS 9–11

At the consecration of the Tabernacle, a divine fire descends to consume the prepared sacrifices that lay upon the altar. When his sons are killed after offering "strange fire," Aaron is not even permitted to grieve. The Torah signifies that if a female Levite married a male Levite, when she died he could not grieve, for the male priests were only allowed to mourn their blood relatives. Since these were his sons, we would expect to hear Aaron's grief. However, he is silent.

Leviticus also provides several guidelines for the use of food, the type of food to be consumed, and its proper preparation. Maintaining the system of strict dietary, or kosher, laws fell upon women. A list of forbidden animals, purity laws, and rules about vessels for cooking and storing food are also included in this part of Leviticus. This entire process is a way of sensitizing the hearts of a nation toward a delivering God. All of the people had to understand the proper conduct of a holy life. These laws teach a respect for all life as well as for the Giver of all life!

> ***Purifying One,*** *take all of me and make me fit for use as Your dwelling place.*

LEVITICUS 12–13

Childbirth and leprosy are placed in the context of ritual purity. "According to the days of the separation for her infirmity shall she be unclean" (Lev. 12:2). This law places certain restrictions upon childbearing women. During a specified period (one week after bearing a son and two weeks after a daughter), a woman is declared ritually impure. She is restricted from her husband's bed and certain religious areas. This time of restriction was due to her "blood defilement," when it was believed that her presence and touch could contaminate others. After birthing and waiting the required time period, a woman had to take both a purification and burnt offering to the priest.

> ***Birthing God,*** *hear the pain of my heart and send Your healing power to comfort me.*

LEVITICUS 14–15

Isolation, sacrificial atonement, and public ritual are required in order to participate in the religious life of the community. However, menstruation, an ongoing and predictable discharge, rendered the average woman impure about one quarter of her life!

> **Life-Giver,** *make my days apart from others more meaningful with You!*

LEVITICUS 16–18

The ritual of atonement is set forth to allow the most holy man in the community to approach God on behalf of all others after sending the scapegoat into the wilderness (Lev. 16:8–22). A bull had to be sacrificed on behalf of the priest, and a goat was offered for the community. These two sin offerings made atonement for the sins of the people. The blood from both animals was used to cleanse the tabernacle and the altar. Once again, we face the paradox of blood both purifying and defiling: "For the life of the flesh is in the blood: and I have given it to you upon the altar to make an atonement for your souls: for it is the blood that maketh an atonement for the soul" (Lev. 17:11).

> **Redeemer,** *thank You for being my ultimate sin offering.*

LEVITICUS 16–18

Chapter 18 details sexual boundaries, including incest, adultery, bestiality, homosexuality, and sexual contact with a menstruating woman. The pharaohs made a practice of marrying their own mothers and sisters. And some of the pagan cults practiced strange sexual couplings. God forbade these practices and regulated the boundaries of sexual contact. In the blending of complex family relationships, it was a safeguard to many women that the boundaries were specifically spelled out. The laws of conduct condemned all adultery, homosexuality, and bestiality.

> **Boundary-Maker,** *thank You for providing for my safety and the safety of my sisters.*

LEVITICUS 19–20

Social, economic, sexual, and ritual conduct are clarified in order to protect weaker members of society: to ensure justice, respect for nature, and preserve the religious codes. The command is given, "Ye shall be holy: for I the Lord your God am holy" (Lev. 19:2). Proper behavior in the community was a mandate. Consequences for unholy behavior are detailed in Leviticus.

Additionally, the practice of body tattoo is addressed in this section: "Ye shall not make any cuttings in your flesh for the dead, or print any marks upon you" (Lev. 19:28). Tattooing was viewed as a foreign custom, often in honor of a cultic god or goddess. Sorcery, magic readings, and communing with spirits are condemned and banned among God's people. Some contemporary female rabbis believe that this particular taboo, repeated three times in 34 verses, was most directly aimed at strong women who were practicing spiritual leadership and threatening the patriarchal authority that was in place. However, the Law states: "And ye shall not walk in the manners of the nation, which I cast out before you: for they committed all these things, and therefore I abhorred them" (Lev. 20:23). Israel was to be a light to the world, not a follower of other countries.

Sanctifying One, make me unique and distinct from the world.

LEVITICUS 21–24

The roles and duties of the priests are also detailed. Holy men were required to marry holy women. The observance of holy days and festivals, including the Sabbath, and observance of special seasons, are outlined. Women were responsible for the preparation of the home—meaning that they had to be familiar with the dietary laws. Specific instructions were outlined regarding the sacred anointing oil and showbread displayed upon the table in the sanctuary.

Bread of Heaven, feed me until I want no more.

LEVITICUS 25–26

"And the sabbath of the land shall be meat for you; for thee, and for thy servant, and for thy maid, and for thy hired servant, and for thy stranger that sojourneth with thee" (Lev. 25:6). The land and its people were to be rested every seven years (Lev. 25:3–4). In a social framework, this allowed all participants to have a fresh start and not to be overburdened by debt (25:6ff.). When the laws were first compiled, women were not permitted to own land or property, or to become heirs, thereby making sabbaticals and jubilee irrelevant to women directly.

LEVITICUS 26–27

God concludes this book of the communal Holiness Codes with both a promise of blessing and shalom (peace) if the people will obey. The promise extends to the land, which is an important part of the covenant. Yet the threat of impending doom is stated firmly: If the people do not follow the laws of conduct as outlined, there will be famine, destruction, and exile.

Blessed Holy One, take my life and let it be, always and forever a praise unto Thee!

NUMBERS LIFE LESSONS

NUMBERS 1–4

The Book of Numbers begins with a census, which was a means of determining who was of arms-bearing age, or who could become a soldier to defend the land promised to God's people. The Levites are exempt due to their sacred roles of the priesthood. Of course in biblical times, women were not counted in this census; but God counted them as His faithful followers. The first chapters are filled with family history, laws, and arrangements for tribal camps.

> **God who counts,** *thank You for counting me in the number, as a warrior for You!*

NUMBERS 5–6

The purity of the camp, restitution for wrongs, the requirements for Nazirites, and the priestly blessing are outlined. Of note to women is the section beginning with Numbers 5:11, where the test for an unfaithful wife is detailed. This is the only example in all of the Bible of a "trial by ordeal." It is a ritual for judging a woman's innocence or guilt by subjecting her to a physical test. During the ritual, the priest places the husband's offering upon his wife's hands, so that she becomes the altar! A bitter potion of dirt and ink is mixed and the woman is to swear her innocence in being unfaithful to her husband. If she is guilty her thighs and abdomen will rot after drinking the potion. "And if the woman be not defiled, but be clean; then she shall be free, and shall conceive seed" (Num. 5:28). Centuries later, Rabbi Yohanan ben Zakkai outlawed this ritual even while the temple was standing because he recognized how destructive marital jealousy could be to the stability of the family.

This section concludes with God's blessing, extended to the people through the priesthood. It was originally given to Moses, passed on to Aaron, and then on to Aaron's sons: "The Lord bless thee, and keep thee: The Lord make his face shine upon thee, and be gracious unto thee: The Lord lift up his countenance upon thee, and give thee peace. And they shall put my name upon the children of Israel; and I will bless them" (Num. 6:24–27).

> **One True Father,** *thank You for bestowing both Your punishments and Your blessings upon us, because only You know what is truly good for us.*

NUMBERS 7–10

This section of Numbers covers the official set up and dedication of the tabernacle; the cloud covering the tabernacle, and the silver trumpets designed for calling the community together and for having the camps set out.

> **Hovering and Calling God,** *let me sense Your presence and know Your voice.*

NUMBERS 12

Miriam and Aaron begin to talk against Moses because of his Cushite wife, Zipporah. It is interesting to note that we find Miriam's name—a woman's—mentioned first. They question his authority as the primary one through whom God speaks to the children of Israel. God demands both of them to step forward at the entrance to the tent. Both are chastised and "the anger of the Lord was kindled against them" (Num. 12:9). However, when the cloud lifted and God was gone, there stood Miriam, white with leprosy! For seven days Miriam was put outside the camp for shame, disgrace, and humiliation. However, Aaron was not punished. One view holds that since Aaron had already lost two sons, the two who offered "strange fire," that this time his punishment was mental. In other words, he was forced to watch his sister suffer for the sin they both committed. Miriam is punished severely for challenging the authority of her brother, whom God had selected as representative and deliverer.

> ***Seeing,*** *Hearing Judge, forgive me when I question those in authority.*

NUMBERS 13–14

Twelve spies are sent out to explore the Promised Land of Canaan. Joshua and Caleb are the only ones to come back with a favorable report: "If the Lord delight in us, then he will bring us into this land, and give it us . . . rebel not ye against the Lord, neither fear ye the people of the land; . . . their defence is departed from them, and the Lord is with us: fear them not," (Num. 14:8–9). The people, however, choose to listen to the negative reports of the other ten spies and rebellion breaks out. Talk of stoning their leaders erupts and God's anger is apparent. The men responsible for spreading the negative reports were struck down by God and die of a plague (Num. 14:37). All the people over 20 years of age are doomed never to see the Promised Land.

__Lord,__ I believe. Help my unbelief! Don't ever let me sell You short!

NUMBERS 16

Korah, a Levite, and certain Reubenites become insolent and rise up against Moses. God threatens to kill the whole assembly except for Moses and Aaron (Num. 16:21). Moses and Aaron beg for the people's lives. God sends earthquakes and consuming fire to rid the camp of rebellion (16:31–35). Fourteen thousand seven hundred people lose their lives from a plague.

__Holy One,__ rid my heart of rebellion!

NUMBERS 20

The death of Miriam is noted. She is buried in the desert of Zin at Kadesh. The record holds that she died on the tenth day of the month of Nisan, 40 years to the day after the Israelites killed the first Passover lamb, and one year before they crossed over into the Promised Land. A day of fasting for women was customary to honor her memory. At the time of her death, there is no water for the community. What a paradox, since she was the girl who stood watch over the waters where her brother was hidden. She was there when Pharaoh's daughter drew her brother from the water and named him. And she walked, along with her brothers, across the dry land of the Red Sea into liberation. Yet she dies in a dry place.

> ***O God,*** *give me living water—water that can quench my soul's thirst for You.*

NUMBERS 21

The children of Israel begin to grumble about the lack of bread and water and their dislike for the food they are receiving from God while in the desert. Because of their complaining, the Lord sends venomous snakes among the people to bite them. Many people die as a result of this (Num. 21:6). The people cry out to Moses in repentance and ask him to pray to the Lord to stop the vicious snake attack. God responds by instructing Moses: "Make thee a fiery serpent, and set it upon a pole: and it shall come to pass, that every one that is bitten, when he looketh upon it, shall live" (Num. 21:8).

> *I will lift up mine eyes unto the hills,* from whence cometh my help. My help cometh from the Lord, which made heaven and earth (Ps. 121:1–2).

NUMBERS 22–24

Here is Balak, Balaam, and the talking jackass. God uses Balaam's donkey to get his attention. What must God use to get our attention?

> *Lord,* thank You for all the special things You do to grab my attention—even dying on a cross.

NUMBERS 25

The men of Israel begin to indulge in sexual immorality with Moabite women who invite them to the sacrificial ceremonies dedicated to their false gods (Num. 25:1–3). This occurs just after Balaam announces the blessings of God upon the people. The people turn away from God to worship idols! One bold sinner (Zimri, a leader of the tribe of Simeon) has the audacity to engage in sexual relations with a Midianite woman (Cozbi, the daughter of the tribal chief Zur) in front of Moses and the entire assembly of Israel (Num. 25:6). Aaron's grandson, Phinehas, becomes so outraged that he kills them both. Twenty-four thousand Israelites are killed by a plague because of their sexual misconduct and whorish acts in seeking after false gods.

> *Jealous God,* help me to worship You and not false gods like money, fame, or sexual depravity.

NUMBERS 27

The daughters of Zelophehad come before Moses with a request to inherit the property that would have been passed on to their father's sons. Because he had been a loyal follower, yet left no sons to inherit, the sisters reasoned that they were due to receive his share of the Promised Land. They petitioned the full assembly—something that had never before been done by women. Moses then brings their case before the Lord, and God agrees with their rationale. A new law was established allowing women to receive inheritances.

> *Gracious God,* give me wisdom so that I may know the blessings in store for me!

NUMBERS 34–35

In these two chapters God establishes specific land boundaries for the Israelites when they enter the land of Canaan. Forty-eight towns are set aside specifically for the Levites, six of which are to be used as places of refuge (Num. 35:6).

Divine Refuge, let me hide under the shelter of Your wings.

NUMBERS 36

Numbers closes with Moses' instructions to the daughters of Zelophehad regarding the inheritance of their father's land: "This is the thing which the Lord doth command concerning the daughters of Zelophehad, saying, Let them marry to whom they think best; only to the family of the tribe of their father shall they marry" (Num. 36:6). The daughters choose to marry their paternal first cousins from the tribe of Manasseh, "And they were married into the families of the sons of Manasseh the son of Joseph, and their inheritance remained in the tribe of the family of their father" (Num. 36:12).

Provider and Protector of Women, please continue to attend to us with gracious care.

DEUTERONOMY LIFE LESSONS

DEUTERONOMY 1–4

Moses tells the people, "The Lord our God spake unto us in Horeb, saying Ye have dwelt long enough in this mount:

Turn you, and take your journey" (Deut. 1:6). The journey from Horeb to Kadesh-barnea was only 11 days (Deut. 1:2). Yet, for over 40 years, 11 months, and 1 day, the Israelites had been stuck in the wilderness (Deut. 1:3). Our inability to trust God and follow God's instructions often puts us in a state of wandering. When we find ourselves in the same place, doing the same thing, and getting the same results while looking for different results, it is most likely God's way of saying, "Move it, girl!"

Moses appointed tribal leaders because he could not continue to govern the people alone. The people suggested that Moses send spies into the valley of Eshcol, and God agreed that this should be done before the people entered the Promised Land. Because the people did not believe that they could defeat the Amorites, they refused to enter. It was because of their disbelief that God allowed only Caleb, Joshua, and the next generation of Israelites to enter the Promised Land.

> *Director of Purpose, help me to move when You say move, so that I do not repeat the same mistakes! I know there is no other God but You, and I want to act on this knowledge.*

DEUTERONOMY 5–6

The Ten Commandments are given to the people with the understanding that God is a jealous God: "I am the Lord your God . . . thou shalt have none other gods before me"

(Deut. 5:6–7). Women today understand and long for a good, loving, and faithful husband. Within the context of marital fidelity, couples vow to have allegiance to just one spouse. The church is referred to as "the bride of Christ" and the marital context continues. The creed, which is drawn from these rules for proper worship and living, stems from God's decree, "I, the Lord your God, am a jealous God."

Thank You for being my Jealous Lord. Help me to stay faithful and true to You and to give You no cause to be jealous.

Although the Ten Commandments address the proper conduct of women (even slaves), it appears that women did not have equality under ancient laws and customs. However, God does include women in the commandments to be faithful and true to God.

Holy One, help me to walk in all the ways You have commanded so that I may live and prosper for many days.

DEUTERONOMY 7

Driving out the established nations that were bigger and stronger than they was the next step for the Israelites in the new land. They were to "utterly destroy them; thou shalt make no covenant with them, nor show mercy unto them"

(Deut. 7:2). The Hittites, Girgasites, Amorites, Canaanites, Perizzites, Hivites, and Jebusites were all descendants of Ham. The observation should be made that these nations were not being punished and disowned by God because they were black, but because they served idols and did not adhere to God's moral code. At any period in history, nations or individuals that reject the moral laws of God will reap the consequences of their behavior. God chooses the time and method: "For thou art an holy people unto the Lord thy God" (Deut. 7:6).

> ***Divine Being,*** *help me expel every idol from my life.*

DEUTERONOMY 8–20

Moses cautions the people not to forget all that God has done for them (Deut. 8:1). Yet, he recalls for them how often they have forgotten God in the past. He reminds them of the golden calf they erected and how he had to receive new tablets containing the Ten Commandments because of their disobedience. He urges them to have reverence for God, to love and obey God, and to remember the place of true worship—the dwelling of God's name. "But unto the place which the Lord your God shall choose... thither thou shalt come, . . ." he said. "And thither ye shall bring your burnt offerings, and your sacrifices, and your tithes... and ye shall rejoice in all that ye put your hand unto... wherein the Lord thy God hath blessed thee" (Deut. 12:5–7). Levitical codes are studied, the jubilee years reinforced, and the occasions of seasons and festivals are detailed. Moses instructs the people to appoint judges who will judge fairly: "That which is altogether just shalt thou follow" (Deut. 16:18–20). The coronation of a king is prophesied (Deut. 17:4–20), and instructions for battle are laid before them: "When thou goest out to battle, be not afraid of them: for the Lord thy God is with thee" (Deut. 20:1).

> **Winning Warrior,** *fight my battles. Let my striving cease.*

DEUTERONOMY 21

The role of women, particularly beautiful, captive women, is discussed (Deut. 21:11–14). It is agreed that women can be acquired during war, for they are part of the warriors' spoils or goods. When captured, a woman's head is shaven, her nails trimmed, and the clothes she wore discarded. Then, she was allowed a month of mourning for all that she lost when captured. It was the hope of the Torah that with a woman's beauty having been shorn and tossed away, the Israelite male would no longer find her attractive enough for marriage. But, if he desired her as a wife, the discarding of all "foreign" identity would make her eligible for marriage and religious conversion. Then, she could not be cast out, mistreated, or sold into slavery, even if the spouse was displeased. It would have been a dishonor to her womanhood.

Father, help me to know that I am always beautiful and worthy in Your eyes.

DEUTERONOMY 22

There was a steep price to be paid for not being a virgin when married. A bloodstained sheet was to be the evidence of virginity. Yet, here again we find much discussion about the issue of a woman's virginity being suspect. It was the father's role to keep his daughter pure. The tradition of rolling a white runner down the aisle before her father escorts the bride down the aisle was started because of this belief. If a man made a charge that his betrothed was not pure, but a bloodstained sheet was produced the next morning, the elders of the city would punish the male for bringing such disrespect upon the father of his bride!

When an accusation such as this was made against a woman, but proven false, three penalties could be levied against the husband: flogging, fines, and forfeiture of his right to ever divorce the woman.

O Protector, safeguard my innocence and defend me against false accusers.

DEUTERONOMY 24–28

Sex for procreation and pleasure is considered both sacred and necessary. The Law positively values sex within the confines of marriage. "When a man hath taken a new wife, he shall not go out to war, neither shall he be charged with any business: but he shall be free at home one year, and shall cheer up his wife which he hath taken" (Deut. 24:5).

The Bible also takes into account the needs of women who happen to be widows or slaves. "When thou cuttest down thine harvest in thy field, and hast forgot a sheaf in the field, thou shalt not go again to fetch it: it shall be for the stranger, for the fatherless, and for the widow: that the Lord thy God may bless thee in all the work of thine hands" (Deut. 24:19).

The Levirate marriage is instituted beginning with Deuteronomy 25:5. A woman who marries into a family must be passed on to the next brother in marriage if the one she marries dies or is killed before having any male heirs. The first male child would actually be the heir of the first husband. This provision made possible the care of the widowed woman and her minor children. Male sons were expected to care for their widowed mothers.

In his third and final address to the people, Moses lifts up the blessings of obedience to the sacred laws: "And it shall come to pass, if thou shalt hearken diligently unto the voice of the Lord thy God, to observe and to do all his commandments which I command thee this day, that the Lord thy God will set thee on high above all nations of the earth: And all these blessings shall come on thee, and overtake thee, if thou shalt hearken unto the voice of the Lord thy God" (Deut. 28:1–2). But the curse of disobedience is also laid before them: "But it shall come to pass, if thou wilt not hearken unto the voice of the Lord thy God, to observe to do all his commandments . . . that all these curses shall come upon thee, and overtake thee: Cursed shalt thou be in the city and . . . in the field. Cursed shall be thy basket and thy store. Cursed shall be the fruit of thy body, and the fruit of thy land . . . Cursed shalt thou be when thou comest in, and cursed shalt thou be when thou goest out" (Deut. 28:15–19).

God views the curse of barrenness and infertility as punishment for wrongdoing. Although this was a curse pronounced upon a nation, we can now understand why women throughout the ages have suffered great emotional suffering when unable to have children. It feels like an individual sin.

> ***God who brings forth life,*** *thank You for the opportunity to birth babies. To continue creation, You have gifted women with the ability to bring forth life. And, You allow us the privilege to birth ideas, visions, dreams, and plans that assist Your people on the journey to completeness. For every birth, we praise Your name.*

DEUTERONOMY 31

This sums up Moses' narrative. The covenant is renewed. Prosperity is again detailed. The people are asked to choose life over death. Joshua is ordained as the new leader. Moses places the written law into the hands of the priests, who place it in the ark of the covenant. He instructs them to read it annually: "Gather the people together, men, and women, and children, and thy stranger that is within thy gates, that they may hear, and that they may learn, and fear the Lord your God, and observe to do all the words of this law" (Deut. 31:12). God tells Moses that the people of Israel will rebel after Moses' death—He foresees their hard hearts and stubborn ways (Deut. 31:14–18).

Dear Faithful One, help me to be faithful to You.

JOSHUA LIFE LESSONS

JOSHUA 1–5

God assures Joshua of success if the words of Moses are adhered to. The spies are sent to "go view the land" (2:1). Upon arrival, they go first into Rahab's home. She risks her life by harboring them and by lying to the authorities about the spies' whereabouts. She requests safety only for herself and her family when the Israelites defeat the Canaanites. The Israelite spies tell her to mark her home by hanging a scarlet cord outside her window (v. 18). Upon the spies' return, the people of Israel cross the Jordan River and take 12 stones to mark the occasion of establishing their home (chaps. 3–4). Since the first generation of Israelites who left Egypt died in the wilderness due to their disobedience, Joshua requires that all males be circumcised again as a reminder of the covenant with God (5:1–8). God states at the conclusion of the ceremony, "This day, have I rolled away the reproach of Egypt from off of you" (Josh. 5:9). Thus begins a new period in their history.

> ***Renewing Covenant Maker,*** *circumcise my hard heart. Give me a heart ready and willing to do Your will.*

JOSHUA 6–12

The walled city of Jericho is well fortified; yet God does not direct Joshua to arm the best-trained warriors for battle. Instead, seven priests carrying trumpets of rams horns in front of the ark of the covenant are to march around the city once a day for six days (6:3–4a). The men of war follow them. On the seventh day, they are to march around the city seven times, with the priests blowing the trumpets. When the people hear the sound of a long blast on the trumpets, they are to give a loud shout. The wall of the city would collapse and the people able to enter (vv. 6:4b–5). All of the possessions of Jericho, with the exception of "silver, and gold, and vessels of brass and iron" are to be destroyed because the people are "accursed" (vv. 18–19). Yet one of the Israelite men, Achan, decided to be disobedient and to take a few keepsakes for himself (chap. 7). His sin caused God's anger to burn against Israel. When Israel began to lose battles, God demanded that Joshua search out the belongings of the entire congregation (vv. 10–24). Achan's disobedience brought death and destruction to all his family (v. 24): "And they raised over him a great heap of stones unto this day. So the Lord turned from the fierceness of his anger" (v. 26). The covenant with the Lord, "as Moses the servant of the Lord commanded" is renewed at Mount Ebal (8:30–34). Later, the sun stands still for a full day while the Israelite warriors battle successfully (10:13). The southern cities are conquered and the northern kings defeated—31 in all (12:24).

Conquering King, win the battles before me. Let Your Son "shine" upon me.

JOSHUA 13–21

The tribes of Israel divide the Promised Land. In the middle of the division we find women who receive property. One of these women is Achsah, the daughter of Caleb—one of the two spies who boldly proclaimed that Israel could take the land during the time of Moses (Num. 13:30; 14:6). "And Caleb said, He that smiteth Kirjath-sepher, and taketh it, to him will I give Achsah my daughter to wife" (15:16). Othniel, son of Kenaz, Caleb's brother, takes it, and receives Achsah as his wife. One day Achsah makes a request of her father: "Give me a blessing; for thou hast given me a south land; give me also springs of water. And he gave her the upper springs, and the nether springs" (v. 19). Joshua 17:3–6 recounts the inheritance of Mahlah, Noah, Hoglah, Milcah, and Tirzah—

the daughters of Zelophehad. The case of the daughters of Zelophehad was a precedent set during the time of Moses (Num. 27:1–11).

> ***God of the marginalized and oppressed,*** *thank You for looking out for the needs of women.*

Joshua 21–24

God's people now inhabit the land of Canaan. Joshua bids farewell to the leaders (chaps. 23–24). The covenant is renewed at Shechem and the people present themselves to the Lord, declaring their faithfulness and allegiance to God after Joshua reminds to make a choice about serving God: "If it seems evil unto you to serve the Lord, choose you this day whom ye will serve; whether the gods which your fathers served that were on the other side of the flood, or the gods of the Amorites, in whose land ye dwell: but as for me and my house, we will serve the Lord" (24:15). And the people said to Joshua, "The Lord our God will we serve, and His voice will we obey" (v. 24). Joshua then dies and is buried in the Promised Land (v. 33).

> ***My God,*** *I will serve You.*

JUDGES LIFE LESSONS

JUDGES 2

Judges 2:1–3 states: "And an angel of the Lord came up from Gilgal to Bochim, and said, I made you to go up out of Egypt, and have brought you unto the land which I sware unto your fathers; and I said, I will never break my covenant with you. And ye shall make no league with the inhabitants of this land; ye shall throw down their altars: but ye have not obeyed my voice: why have ye done this? Wherefore I also said, I will not drive them out from before you; but they shall be as thorns in your sides, and their gods shall be a snare unto you." This proclamation sets the stage for Israel to be oppressed by its enemies in the Promised Land.

***Covenant Maker**, help me discover and then destroy every idol in my life so that You alone may rule.*

"Nevertheless, the Lord raised up judges, which delivered them out of the hand of those that spoiled them. And yet they would not hearken unto their judges, but they went a whoring after other gods, and bowed themselves unto them: they turned quickly out of the way which their fathers walked in, obeying the commandments of the Lord; but they did not so. And when the Lord raised them up judges, then the Lord was with the judge, and delivered them out of the hand of their enemies all the days of the judge: for it repented the Lord because of their groanings by reason of them that oppressed them and vexed them. And it came to pass, when the judge was dead, that they returned, and corrupted themselves more than their fathers, in following other gods to serve them, and to bow down unto them; they ceased not from their own doings, nor from their stubborn ways. And the anger of the Lord was hot against Israel" (2:16–20).

The first judge is Othniel, son of Kenaz, Caleb's younger brother (3:9). Othniel also is the spouse of Achsah (1:11–15). Ehud becomes the second judge (3:15–30), and Shamgar the third (v. 31). When Israel continues to do evil, God acts: "And the Lord sold them into the hand of Jabin king of Canaan, that reigned in Hazor; . . . and the children of Israel cried unto the Lord . . . twenty years he mightily oppressed the children of Israel" (4:2–3).

> *Great Savior, deliver me from my repeated sinful cycles. Allow me to hear the voices of those who come with words of salvation. Turn Your anger from me that I may live an abundant life.*

JUDGES 4-5

"Deborah, a prophetess, the wife of Lapidoth, she judged Israel at that time. And she dwelt under the palm tree of Deborah between Ramah and Beth-el in mount Ephraim: and the children of Israel came up to her for judgment. And she sent and called Barak" (4:4–6). It is interesting to note that Deborah is introduced as the wife of Lapidoth, whose name means "son of fire." So we might call her the "wife" or "woman of fire," although she stays close to home, doing what she has to do. Her husband's character, position, and deeds are not part of the record. We should not conclude that her role as wife is less important than her role as judge. As both prophet and judge, she has a relationship with Israel that is both religious and judicial. And, she is referred to as a "mother in Israel" (5:7). While we have not seen a primary female leader in Israel, Deborah could be perceived as "nursemaid to a politically incapacitated Israel" (WBC, 69). All that she learned as a girl to prepare her for womanhood, God now wants her to use in her role as judge.

When she summons a military commander, Barak comes. She gives him a word from the Lord—marching orders after twenty years of military oppression. But God's intention is to save Israel under the leadership of a judge, not military might. Barak is not opposed to going, but will only go if Deborah agrees to go with him. Deborah replies: "I will surely go with thee: notwithstanding the journey that thou takest shall not be for thine honour; for the Lord shall sell Sisera into the hand of a woman" (4:9). Deborah goes with

Barak and 10,000 men to Kedesh (v. 10). Warrior Deborah goes into battle, and the hand of the saving and delivering God is with Israel.

> ***Reliable Deliverer,*** *I magnify Your great name for choosing me to do work worthy of You. Help me know that You can choose a woman to win the war for Your people. Thank You for being the God who never fails!*

Sisera, commander of the Canaanite army, witnessed the destruction of his army at the hands of less skilled Israelites. He escapes on foot, seeking asylum in the tent of Hazor of the Heber clan. Because of their alliance, he feels secure entering Hazor's tent and making demands of Hazor's wife, Jael. Jael has more pressing matters to consider than an obsolete political alliance between her husband and this defeated commander. She is clearly a woman caught in the middle.

Jael welcomes Sisera and treats him with maternal care. When he falls asleep, assured of his safety, she drives a tent peg through his head, leaving him to die. Jael not only wins her security; but in the song of Deborah and Barak, she wins Israel's praise as well (5:24–27). In their description of Jael's feat, her violent act becomes larger than life. Sisera had mistaken Jael's womanhood and kindness for weakness. He did not understand that God could use a woman. God had used Deborah to establish 40 years of peace in Israel (v. 31).

> *Equipping God,* let me use the ways You have given me to bring down the unholy giants in my life.

JUDGES 6–8

"The Lord is with thee, thou mighty man of valour," says the angel of the Lord to Gideon, who hides from the Midianites in a winepress (6:12). God chooses Gideon, a man who is afraid to lead Israel, to be a judge. Gideon responds: "Oh my Lord, if the Lord be with us, why then is all this befallen us?" (v. 13). God does not answer this question, but summons Gideon to come out of hiding and "go in this thy might, and thou shalt save Israel from the hand of the Midianites: have not I sent thee?" (v. 14).

Gideon leads Israel in defeating the Midianites: "Thus was Midian subdued before the children of Israel, so that they lifted up their heads no more. And the country was in quietness forty years in the days of Gideon" (8:28).

> *Challenging God,* if You can use a scared individual who is trying diligently to hide from the enemies of life, You can use me.

JUDGES 11

"Now Jephthah the Gileadite was a mighty man of valour, and he was the son of an harlot: and Gilead begat Jephthah" (11:1). Because of his mother's past, Jephthah is exiled from town, only to be sought in later years to command the army against the oppressive Ammonites: "Then Jephthah went with the elders of Gilead, and the people made him head and captain over them: and Jephthah uttered all his words before the Lord in Mizpeh" (v. 11). Wanting assurance of victory (and the town's continued acceptance), Jephthah makes a vow to God: "If thou shalt without fail deliver the children of Ammon into mine hands, then it shall be, that whatsoever cometh forth of the doors of my house to meet me . . . shall surely be the Lord's, and I will offer it up for a burnt offering" (vv. 30–31). His daughter pays the ultimate price for Israel's victory. Although we cannot be certain of the exact nature of the vow, the words of verse 31 are telling.

Jephthah does not specify what he expects to greet him on his arrival. Custom would have created the expectation that a slave or servant would greet the returning victor and master. So, the vow could have meant, more than likely, a servant would have been the sacrifice. Yet Jephthah does not anticipate that his daughter would greet him. Perhaps because of Yahweh, the daughter, whose name we never learn, responds, "Do to me according to that which hath proceeded out of thy mouth" (v. 36).

She then takes matters into her own hands and requests two months "that I may go up and down upon the mountains, and bewail my virginity, I and my fellows" (v. 37). She spends her remaining days with others like herself, who know what life is like in a violent society and who, in the end, will not forget her sacrifice. After she returns to be sacrificed, she becomes a martyr in Israel. Whereas the song of Deborah recounts the deeds of a mighty God, the words of Jephthah's daughter describe the tragic end to the life of a girl, sacrificed needlessly because of her father's desire for a victory that God had already guaranteed by His presence (v. 29). From her short life comes the custom "that the daughters of Israel went yearly to lament the daughter of Jephthah the Gileadite four days in a year" (v. 40).

Lord, prepare me to be a living sacrifice!

JUDGES 13–16

The narrator relates the story of the birth of Samson to Manoah and his wife, who is not named. She is the one to whom the angel appears with the words of pronouncement and instructions for her infant to be set apart by God to begin the deliverance of Israel from the hands of the Philistines (13:3–5). Even when her husband demands an angelic reappearance due to both their long years of childlessness and his unbelief in a "woman's tale," the angel reappears to the wife (v. 9). Here, we see a foreshadowing of the story of Elisabeth, Zacharias, and the foretold coming of John the Baptist (see Luke 1). The child is born to begin the deliverance of the Israelites. They name him Samson (13:24).

Samson is a young man without boundaries. From the beginning we find him enchanted with the wrong women. He says to his parents, "I have seen a woman in Timnath of the daughters of the Philistines; now therefore get her for me to wife" (14:2).

"Loving a Philistine woman, spending his time in wine country, handling dead carcasses and eating unclean food hardly bode well for a Nazarite who is to be Israel's champion against the Philistines" (WBC, 72). Samson breaks all the rules. He does not become a military hero because Israel does not fight the Philistines. They have been oppressed for so long until it seems "their lot." At one point, when he has taken revenge upon the enemy, the men of Judah say to Samson, "Knowest thou not that the Philistines are rulers over us? what is this that thou hast done unto us?" (15:11). What is God to do with people who have no desire to be liberated from their oppressors?

It is only fair to recount that Samson's "rule-breaking" always seems to involve a type of woman not known as a "good Jewish girl"! His first wife is a Philistine, although his parents warn him of God's command against intermarriage, which leads to idol worship (14:1–3; see also Exodus 34:11–16; Numbers 25; Deuteronomy 7:3–4; Joshua 23:12; Judges 3:6; Ezra 9:1–2). Samson also frequents prostitutes (Judg. 16:1). In this we meet Delilah. We know her as the one responsible for Samson's ultimate downfall.

Mighty men in the community come and offer Delilah great wealth, for Samson has fallen in love with her, a fact that is no secret to the community (v. 4). "And the lords of the Philistines came up unto her, and said unto her, Entice him, and see wherein his great strength lieth, and by what means we may prevail against him . . . and we will give thee every one of us eleven hundred pieces of silver" (v. 5).

Samson loves Delilah, but Delilah abandons the love of a hunted man, for the security of wealth (vv. 6–20).

Jehovah-Jireh, may my security come from You.

JUDGES 17

Micah steals 1,100 shekels from his mother and confesses that he has stolen them. She then blesses him (17:1–2). When he gives his mother the money, she declares, "I had wholly dedicated the silver unto the Lord from my hand for my son, to make a graven image and a molten image" (v. 3). The very things that God has forbidden—idols—are built and enshrined in the home of an Israelite. "And the man Micah had an house of gods, and made an ephod, and teraphim, and consecrated one of his sons, who became his priest" (v. 5). Private shrines to idols and priests not sanctioned by God show the great disdain that is now widespread in Israel. This mother-and-son story shows us how people of God, without close relationships with Him, will seek religious security in the same manner as their foreign neighbors.

Encountering One, let me always walk close with You.

JUDGES 19–21

The final Judges story also involves a woman and a Levite. "By focusing on Levites in the concluding episodes, the narrator communicates the extent of Israel's moral decline. The corruption that has infected the people and their deliverers has spread even to those who are entrusted with keeping Yahwistic tradition" (WBC, 75). This story is one of marital discord in which the Levite took a concubine from Bethlehem in Judah who was unfaithful to him, and returns her to her father's house. After four months, the Levite goes to bring her back. On the way home, unwilling to stay another night, the man leaves and goes toward Jerusalem with his two saddled donkeys and his concubine (19:1–2, 10). It is here that trouble begins. An older man from the hill country of Ephraim, living in the area of the Benjamites, invites the group to spend the night at his home. While they are enjoying themselves, some of the wicked men of the city surround the house. Pounding on the door, they shout to the Levite's host, "Bring forth the man that came unto thine house, that we may know him" (v. 22). In other words, the men proposed to have sex with him. The older man counters with another proposition: "Behold, here is my daughter, a maiden, and his concubine; them I will bring out now, and humble ye them, and do with them what seemeth good unto you; but unto this man do not so vile a thing" (v. 24). The men refuse this offer. Nevertheless, the Levite sends out his concubine (v. 25).

The following morning, after the men have violated the concubine, she crawls back to the house from whence she came. There she dies. The Levite picks her up, places her on his donkey, and heads for home. When he reaches home, he takes a knife and cuts the body of his concubine into twelve parts and sends them into all of the areas of Israel (vv. 27-29). The deed is described thusly: "There was no such deed done nor seen from the day that the children of Israel came up out of the land of Egypt unto this day" (v. 30).

Like a sacrificial animal, riding upon a donkey, and sent piece by piece to every tribe of Israel, this nameless woman speaks in profound ways she has not spoken throughout the narrative. Her abused body speaks to all of Israel about abandonment, rejection, and betrayal of those who should have been her protectors. Her sacrificed body is a signal sent by the Levite that his rights have been violated by the Benjamites. "Judah goes up first, not against a foreign enemy, but against other Israelites. The dismemberment is not that of an enemy king, but of an innocent and unprotected Israelite woman. The woman on a donkey rides not erect and determined to secure life, but she is limp and immobile, a victim of violence, the embodiment of betrayal and death" (WBC, 76). The slaughter continues and entire villages are ravished, for violence always begets violence (Judg. 20-21).

The narrator is quick to remind us that "in those days there was no king in Israel, but every man did that which was right in his own eyes" (17:6). The book progresses, and the violence becomes increasingly personal. From the progress of the nation (1:1-26) to the defense of the nation (4:1-5:31) to personal vengeance (14:1-16:31) to the wounded honor of the dishonorable (19:1–20:7), violence is no longer used as a tool for the common good, but as a weapon of anarchy.

God of new beginnings, help me learn from the lessons of yesterday. Let me be better because of my yesterdays.

RUTH
LIFE LESSONS

RUTH 1

We enter the scene in Moab, where there is a complex social situation involving gender issues, marital relationships, travel, and a growing sense of hopelessness. Today, Naomi would be classified as "depressed." First of all, her husband dies; he is followed in death by both of her sons. She has no male kinsmen close by. She is head of a household in which there are three widowed, childless women. Bitter and discouraged, she pronounces, "Call me not Naomi, call me Mara: for the Almighty hath dealt very bitterly with me. I went out full, and the Lord hath brought me home again empty" (1:20–21). She is afraid, for she realizes that she is a woman without resources for survival. Naomi was at rock bottom. She felt that there was nowhere else to go, so she decided to return to her home, Bethlehem.

Hope of the Hopeless, life is bitter. But You alone can make it better.

Naomi kisses Orpah and Ruth and wishes them well: "Go, return each to her mother's house: the Lord deal kindly with you, as ye have dealt with the dead, and with me. The Lord grant you that ye may find rest, each of you in the house of her husband"(1:8–9). Naomi, Ruth, and Orpah are at a crossroads. They each know the past, but they don't have a clue as to what lies ahead. Naomi wishes that each of her daughters-in-law will find new husbands and have children. These are the requirements for a woman's survival in ancient Palestine.

Ruth declared, "Intreat me not to leave thee, or to return from following after thee: for whither thou goest, I will go; and where thou lodgest, I will lodge: thy people shall be my people, and thy God my God: Where thou diest, will I die . . . and more also, if ought but death part thee and me" (vv. 16–17). In marriage the covenant is sealed with binding words. Ruth, a Gentile, is ready to forsake her homeland, her customs, and her gods. She is willing to risk binding her life with Naomi's. She is committed to taking care of another woman who has cared for her in days past. Declaring her intent, the women set out for Bethlehem.

Covenant relationships are not about equality. Covenant relationships are not about "What's in it for me?" Covenant relationships are about serving and meeting the needs of others. These women do not have blood ties to hold them together. They are not even of the same ethnic group. Yet Naomi and Ruth shared love and the common desire to survive.

> *Holy One,* guide me along the way. With You beside me, I cannot stray.

RUTH 2–3

It is Ruth's turn to take the initiative, and take the initiative she does! "And Ruth the Moabite, said unto Naomi, Let me now go to the field, and glean ears of corn after him in whose sight I shall find grace... and her hap was to light on a part of the field belonging unto Boaz, who was of the kindred of Elimelech" (2:2–3). "Then said Boaz unto his servant that was set over the reapers, Whose damsel is this?... It is the Moabitish damsel that came back with Naomi out of the country of Moab" (vv. 5–6). It is important to note that unlike Naomi, the narrative refers to Ruth by speaking of her ethnicity and not her name.

> *Harvester God,* thank You for including me, an outsider, in the sweep of Your vast field.

Boaz arranges for Ruth to remain in his field (2:8–10). He readily becomes her protector, including her in his field crew. She is able to feed and care for both herself and Naomi as she had sworn. "Blessed be he that did take knowledge of thee" (v.19) cries Naomi upon Ruth's return. "Blessed be the of the Lord!" (v.20). Ruth tells Naomi that his name is Boaz.

It takes Naomi only minutes to recall that Boaz is a distant relative of her dead husband. "The man is near of kin unto us, one of our next kinsmen" (v.20).

By definition, a redeemer is one who retains or reclaims a property through purchase, thereby relieving oneself or another from obligation, lien, or slavery. Accordingly, it also reflects God's activity as the Deity who saves from sin, slavery, exile, and death. For Naomi, men function as representatives of heaven on earth (WBC, 81–82). Naomi recognizes the potential role of Boaz as a divinely guided redeemer who, as a relative of her husband, can reclaim the property that she could not. "So she kept fast by the maidens of Boaz to glean unto the end of barley harvest and of wheat harvest; and dwelt with her mother –in law" (2:23). The roles of women supporting each other and working together is depicted as essential for survival.

> *Friend of the Friendless,* grant me supportive community among my sisters.

RUTH 4

Ruth and Boaz marry and live happily ever after. Ruth then gives birth to a son, Obed. The women in the community tell Naomi, "Blessed be the Lord, which hath not left thee this day without a kinsman, that his name may be famous in Israel. And he shall be unto thee a restorer of thy life, and a nourisher of thine old age: for thy daughter-in-law, which loveth thee, which is better to thee than seven sons, hath born him" (4:14–15). Obed later becomes the father of Jesse, who is later the father of David. So a Moabite woman becomes part of the genealogy of Jesus Christ because she kept her covenant. Ruth's story is a true love story.

It is interesting to note that although the book is called Ruth, it ends with Naomi. She who was "empty" cares for the child. The women who greet them upon their arrival in Bethlehem name the child (v. 17).

> ***Dear God,*** *give me the name and identity that You have for me, even in a foreign land.*

1 SAMUEL LIFE LESSONS

1 SAMUEL 1

First Samuel begins with the pain of a barren woman, Hannah, who believes in the power of prayer. Hannah is married to Elkanah, who also has a second wife, Peninnah. Peninnah is a constant source of vexation to Hannah. The family annually made a journey to Shiloh for worship and sacrifice. The context is set with these words: "But unto Hannah he gave a worthy portion; for he loved Hannah: but the Lord had shut up her womb . . . her adversary also provoked her sore... because the Lord had shut up her womb. And... he did so year by year" (1 Sam. 1:5–7). Yet Hannah was persistent in prayer. She had taken a stand with God and was relentless in her desire for a son. Her vow, made at the tabernacle, was even misunderstood by the high priest, who thought she was a drunk. "And it came to pass, as she continued praying before the Lord, that Eli marked her mouth. Now Hannah, she spake in her heart; only her lips moved, but her voice was not heard: therefore Eli thought she had been drunken" (vv. 12–13). But she petitioned until God agreed that the time was right: "Elkanah knew Hannah his wife, and the Lord remembered her" (v. 19).

> ***Petition Grantor,*** *I lay my heart's desire before You.*

1 SAMUEL 2–4

After the consecration of her son, Samuel, Hannah's prayer of thanksgiving is recorded in 1 Samuel 2. When she keeps her promise and takes him to the tabernacle, Eli's poor judgment over his sons' sin is made known. Eli's sons are described as wicked men who had no regard for the Lord (2:12). For this cause God ceases speaking to Eli. But Hannah takes Samuel to the Tabernacle where he is trained by Eli to be a priest. But God speaks to Samuel regarding Eli's house: "And Samuel grew, and the Lord was with him, and did let none of his words fall to the ground. And all Israel from Dan even to Beersheba knew that Samuel was established to be a prophet of the Lord . . . And the word of Samuel came to all Israel" (3:19–4:1).

Later the Philistines capture the ark of the covenant (4:11). Eli dies when he learns of his sons' deaths. His daughter-in-law, the wife of Phinehas, was pregnant at the time. Overcome with grief from the death of her husband and father-in-law, she goes into labor. As she is about to die she names the child Ichabod, meaning "the glory has departed from Israel" (vv. 21–22).

> *Hovering Presence,* don't leave us. We long to hear from You.

1 SAMUEL 7–17

The ark remains at Kirjath-jearim a long time (20 years in all). All the people of Israel mourn and seek the Lord (1 Sam. 7:2). Samuel subdues the Philistines at Mizpah and builds a stone memorial, naming it Ebenezer, saying, "Hitherto hath the Lord helped us" (1 Sam. 7:12). Samuel continues as judge over Israel all the days of his life, and builds an altar to the Lord at Ramah (vv. 15–17).

The people ask Samuel to appoint a king to lead them. The Lord tells him, "Hearken unto the voice of the people in all that they say unto thee: for they have not rejected thee, but they have rejected me" (8:7). Saul is chosen as king in chapter 9, then anointed in chapter 10. In chapter 11, Saul crushes the Ammonites. Chapter 12 shows Samuel bidding farewell to the nation, and in chapter 13, Samuel rebukes Saul, who takes it upon himself to do the ministry of the priest. In chapter 13, Samuel warns Saul that his kingdom will be taken away because of his (Saul's) disobedience. Saul's son, Jonathan, attacks the Philistines in chapter 14. The Lord rejects Saul as king in chapter 15. Chapter 16 shows Samuel anointing David, who kills Goliath in chapter 17. Saul jealousy of David prevails and he tries to kill him, which keeps David on the run (see chapters 18–28).

> ***Abiding God,*** *please don't take Your Holy Spirit away from me!*

1 SAMUEL 25–31

David encounters Nabal and his wife Abigail. She prevents David from shedding innocent blood, and he takes her and Ahinoam of Jezreel to be his wives. Abigail shows us how to prevent the loss of lives. Saul has given his daughter, Michal (another of David's wives) to Phalti, a man from Gallim (25:43–44).

David spares Saul's life and hides from him among the Philistines (chap. 27). "Now Samuel was dead, and all Israel had lamented him, and buried him in Ramah, even in his own city. And Saul had put away those that had familiar spirits, and the wizards, out of the land" (28:3). Saul then further disobeys God by seeking out a medium in Endor who summons up the spirit of Samuel (28:3–25). David is triumphant against the Philistines and the Amalekites (chaps. 29–30). Saul kills himself (chap. 31).

Giver of Wisdom, give me the wisdom of Abigail as I wrestle with fools.

2ND SAMUEL LIFE LESSONS

2 SAMUEL 1–6

Second Samuel continues the story of Israel's monarchy. Second Samuel 1 finds David lamenting the deaths of Saul and Jonathan. David is anointed king over Judah (chap. 2). Second Samuel 3 details the politics of marriage, as David's sons are listed along with the names of their mothers' political lineage. "In addition to Michal, Abigail, Ahinoam, and Bathsheba, 2 Samuel 5:13 notes that David took more concubines and wives. The purpose of these marriages would have been largely political, in order to forge relationships with neighboring kingdoms as with Maacah, the daughter of the king of Gershur and mother of Absalom" (W B C, 92). David welcomes Mephibosheth, the son of Jonathan, into his home and family. Jonathan, son of Saul, had a son who was lame in both feet. He was five years old when news about Saul and Jonathan came from Jezreel. His nurse picked him up and fled, but as she hurried to leave, he fell and became crippled (2 Sam. 4:4). David becomes king over all Israel and conquers Jerusalem (chap. 5). The ark of the covenant is returned to Jerusalem and David dances joyfully. Michal, watching from a window, despises David in her heart (6:16).

> ***Sovereign One,*** *use me in Your service to bring forth good fruit.*

2 SAMUEL 11–12

David's relations with Bathsheba are recounted in 2 Samuel 11–12. David sends messengers to get her, has sex with her, then sends her home. When David receives word that Bathsheba has conceived, he tries to cover up the sin by having her husband, Uriah, sleep with his wife. When Uriah refuses to cooperate with this deception (which is unknown to him), David has Uriah placed in the front line of battle where he is killed. Now Bathsheba is pregnant and widowed at the hand of the king (11:2–17). "And when the mourning was past, David sent and fetched her to his house, and she became his wife, and bare him a son. But the thing that David had done displeased the Lord" (v. 27).

> ***All Knowing and All Seeing God,*** *see those who would harm me. And, let me see those I have harmed.*

2 SAMUEL 12

The prophet Nathan comes and rebukes David with the story of a rich man, a poor man, and one little pet lamb. David points the finger of blame at himself. However, God announces the judgment: "The Lord also hath put away thy sin; thou shalt not die. Howbeit, because by this deed thou hast given great occasion to the enemies of the Lord to blaspheme, the child also that is born unto thee shall surely die" (12:13–14).

> *Maestro of Voiceless Melodies,* catch the perfect pitch of my broken heart.

2 SAMUEL 13–20

The sin of the father affects his household. In 2 Samuel 13, Amnon, son of David, falls in love with his sister Tamar, then rapes her. "Nay, my brother, do not force me; for no such thing ought to be done in Israel: do not thou this folly. And I, whither shall I cause my shame to go?" (13:12–13). Her pleas are to no avail. Her brother, Absalom, kills Amnon and flees. Sin always brings division. In chapter 14, a wise woman of Tekoa is approached to talk to David about restoring harmony in his house. Absalom is sent for, but conspires to take his father's throne. Second Samuel 15–19 tells of the murder of Absalom and David's regret and return to Jerusalem. All of the men of Israel deserted David to follow Sheba, son of Beliel. But the men of Judah stayed by their king (20:2).

Another wise woman speaks to the commander of the army in 2 Samuel 20:16, providing wise counsel.

> ***Ancient of Days,*** *speak Your words of wise counsel through me.*

2 SAMUEL 21

A mother's faithfulness even after her son's death is recounted with the heartrending story of Rizpah, Saul's wife. For a sin Saul had committed against the Gibeonites, her two sons—along with the five sons of Saul's oldest daughter, Merab—were killed and exposed on a hill before the Lord. All seven of them fell together and were put to death during the first days of the harvest: "Rizpah, the daughter of Aiah, took sackcloth and spread it for her upon the rock, from the beginning of harvest until water dropped upon them out of heaven, and suffered neither the birds of the air to rest on them by day, nor the beasts of the field by night" (21:10). It is a love story at its best. As a committee of one, she stayed for six months, keeping vigil over decaying flesh. When the rains came, David gave the boys a decent burial.

> ***Merciful God,*** *send Your refreshing rains to fall down on me and my seeming decay. I wait for the latter rains.*

2 SAMUEL 22–24

In these chapters, we see the days of David draw to an end.

Mighty God, You have raised up a mighty nation and a great king. Now raise me and allow me to serve Your sovereign name!

1 KINGS LIFE LESSONS

1 KINGS 1–3

First Kings 1 introduces us to a dying King David. As factions rise to take the kingdom, David calls Bathsheba and promises the kingdom to their son, Solomon (1:28–31). In 1 Kings 2, Solomon is made king. David's son Adonijah, by Haggith, decided that he should be king instead and went to seek Bathsheba's help in securing Abishag, a Shunammite who took care of David, for his wife. She intervenes with Solomon, who in turn decides that Adonijah should be put to death for being so forward. With the kingdom firmly established, Solomon asks for wisdom to guide the people of God (3:1–15).

Two prostitutes who come to Solomon seeking judgment immediately put his wisdom to the test (vv. 16–28). "This story's primary purpose is to establish the wisdom of Solomon, yet it provides insight into the lives of prostitutes in Israelite culture and into the humanity of all people, even those despised by society. The opening scene is arresting in its simple statement that two prostitutes can approach the king. The ability of people of such low social standing to have an audience with the king demonstrates the narrator's belief that Solomon was a champion of all Israelites" (The Storyteller's Companion, 142).

> *Compassionate God,* give me a discerning spirit to know how to do what is just.

1 KINGS 7–11

In 1 Kings 7–10, Solomon builds the temple. The queen of Sheba hears of his wisdom and travels a great distance to test him with hard questions (1 Kin. 10:3). The queen is presented as one empowered to accredit others as having wisdom. She confirms Solomon's wisdom and presents him with riches and honor.

King Solomon, however, takes many foreign women as wives. They are from nations about which the Lord had told the Israelites, "Ye shall not go in to them, neither shall they come in unto you: for surely they will turn away your heart after their gods: Solomon clave unto these in love" (11:2). God raised up adversaries against Solomon in Hadad the Edomite (v. 14) and Jeroboam, son of Nebat (v. 26).

God declares to Jeroboam, "I will not take the whole kingdom out of his hand: but I will make him prince all the days of his life for David my servant's sake ... But I will take the kingdom out of his son's hand, and will give it unto thee, even ten tribes. And unto his son will I give one tribe, that David my servant may have a light alway before me in Jerusalem, the city which I have chosen me to put my name there" (vv. 34–36). Solomon tries to kill Jeroboam, but Jeroboam flees to Egypt and remains there until Solomon's death. Solomon's son Rehoboam succeeds him as king (vv. 41–43).

> ***Loving and Enabling God,*** *keep me from that which is foreign to You and Your ways.*

1 KINGS 12–16

The kingdom is divided. Jeroboam does evil in God's sight by setting up idols and saying to Israel, "It is too much for you to go up to Jerusalem: behold thy gods, O Israel, which brought thee up out of the land of Egypt ... And this thing became a sin: for the people went to worship before the one, even unto Dan" (12:25–33). Jeroboam's son becomes ill, which prompts him to have his unnamed wife disguise herself and go to Shiloh to see Ahijah, the prophet of God (14:1–18). God warns Ahijah that the woman is coming. Ahijah does not allow her to keep up the pretense with him at all. He declares to her that because of the wickedness of her husband, her son will die as soon as she sets foot in the city!

"The Lord shall raise him up a king over Israel, who shall cut off the house of Jeroboam that day...For the Lord shall smite Israel, as a reed is shaken in the water . . . because of the sins of Jeroboam, who did sin, and who made Israel" (vv. 14–16). Harsh punishment is pronounced upon the house of Jeroboam (vv. 10–12). And after twenty-two years as king, Jeroboam dies (v. 20).

Rehoboam, son of Solomon and Naamah, his Ammonite wife, rules in Judah as king. There is continual warfare between Rehoboam and Jeroboam until Rehoboam dies and his son, Abijam, succeeds him (14:21–31). Abijam's heart is not fully devoted to the Lord (15:3). There is war between Abijam and Jeroboam until Abijam dies and his son Asa succeeds him (v. 8). Asa rules for forty-one years. Asa does what is right in the eyes of the Lord (vv. 9–11). He even deposes his mother, Maacah (daughter of Abishalom), from her position as Queen Mother because of her idolatry (v. 13). Asa dies and his son, Jehoshaphat, succeeds him (v. 24). Nadab, the son of Jeroboam, becomes king of Israel. He does evil in the sight of the Lord (vv. 25–26). Baasha kills Nadab in the third year and becomes king (v. 28). He also does evil in the sight of the Lord (v. 34). When Baasha dies, his son, Elah, succeeds him (1 King 16:6). Elah's servant Zimri strikes down Elah and succeeds him as king (v. 10). Zimri's reign lasts seven days. He then dies because of the sins he had committed (v. 19). The people of Israel are then split into two factions: half support Tibni son of Ginath and the other half support Omri. Omri becomes king of Israel, but does evil in the sight of the Lord (vv. 21–25). When he dies, his son, Ahab, became king (v. 28).

Holy One, guard my heart. Keep me from doing evil in Your sight.

1 KINGS 17–22

Chapter 17 introduces us to Elijah the Tishbite, who is called by God to tell Ahab, "As the Lord God of Israel liveth, before whom I stand, there shall not be dew nor rain these few years but according to my word" (17:1). Elijah is instructed to go to the brook Cherith (v. 3), east of the Jordan, where a miracle occurs—ravens feed him until the brook dries up. God sends Elijah to a widow in Zarephath because she obeyed Elijah's word. "Fear not; go and do as thou hast said: but make me thereof a little cake first, and bring it unto me, and after make for thee and for they son. For thus saith the Lord God of Israel, The barrel of meal shall not waste, neither shall the cruse of oil fail, until the day that the Lord sendeth rain upon the earth" (vv. 13–14). When the widow's son suddenly dies, she calls out to Elijah. The Lord hears Elijah's cry, and the boy is revived (v. 22).

Chapter 18 finds the land in its third year of famine. We are introduced to Ahab's wife, Jezebel—a Phoenician princess: "Now Obadiah feared the Lord greatly: For it was so, when Jezebel cut off the prophets of the Lord, that Obadiah took an hundred prophets, and hid them by fifty in a cave" (v. 4). Jezebel is a worshiper of Baal, which sets her at odds with

God's prophets, particularly Elijah. In Chapter 18, she sends a messenger to Elijah stating, "So let the gods do to me, and more also if I make not thy life as the life of one of them by to morrow about this time." Elijah escapes to avoid death, but first performs a feat displaying God's power on Mount Carmel.

Elijah flees to Horeb (chap. 19) where the Lord appears to him. Ben-hadad attacks Samaria but Ahab defeats him (chap. 20) and is condemned to death by a prophet. In chapter 21, Ahab longs for Naboth's vineyard and Jezebel asks, "Doest thou now govern the kingdom of Israel? arise, and eat bread, and let thine heart be merry: I will give thee the vineyard of Naboth the Jezreelite" (v. 7).

Jezebel's perverted leadership results in her death and that of Ahab. "Thus saith the Lord, In the place where dogs licked the blood of Naboth shall dogs lick thy blood, even this" (v. 19) And concerning Jezebel, the Lord says, 'Dogs will devour Jezebel by the wall of Jezreel' " (v. 23). Ahab dies and his son Ahaziah takes the throne (22:40).

2ND KINGS LIFE LESSONS

2 KINGS 2–8

The divided kingdom continues. Elijah passes on the mantle of faith to Elisha when he is taken up to heaven in a whirlwind (2:1–12). Joram, son of Ahab, becomes king. The Scriptures describe him thusly: "He wrought evil in the sight of the Lord" (3:2). The wife of a prophet approaches Elisha with the news that her sons will be sold into slavery to repay a debt (4:1). The power of God in Elisha is verified as the miracle of oil flows to fill enough jars for the widow to pay her debts and make enough money to survive (vv. 2–7). Later we find a wealthy woman in Shunem who makes a place for the "holy man of God" (vv. 9–10). When Elisha sends his servant Gahazi to ask what can be done to pay for the hospitality, the woman asks for nothing! So Elisha prophesies that a son would be born to her and her aged spouse. One day her son dies. She goes straight to the Elisha and demands, "Did I desire a son of my lord? did I not say, Do not deceive me?" (v. 28) Elisha goes home with the distraught mother and the son is restored to life (v. 36). In chapter eight, we find the miracle of this woman's land being restored by the king after her seven years of exile. "Give back everything that belonged to her, including all the income from her land from the day she left the country until now" (8:6). Her faith has made her whole.

Granting Lord, restore unto me all that the enemy has stolen.

2 KINGS 5

Chapter five tells of the miracle of forgiveness in a young woman who helps the same military leader who captured her from her homeland and made her his wife's servant. The chapter is a testament to love at work in a foreign land. The young woman remains nameless; however, the narrator does provide some insight into her station in life. Naaman has leprosy, which would entail his forfeiting his military rank and position and going to live in the leper's camp. When the young woman discovers his secret, she tells his wife of the prophet, Elisha. Naaman is sent by the king to visit Elisha, who heals him when he dips seven times in the Jordan. Thanks to the nameless woman, Naaman discovers the power of the Lord.

Namer of the Nameless, name me "Love."

2 KINGS 6–11

Jezebel, with temptation and idolatry in her heart, meets her foretold doom in chapter nine: "So they threw her down: and some of her blood was sprinkled on the wall, and on the horses: and he trode her underfoot" (v. 33). Jezebel's downfall does not come about because of the way she wears makeup, fixes her hair, or uses charcoal upon her eyes. She is cursed when she decides that Baal is more powerful than the Living God is! Worshiping an idol that has no power caused her death.

Chapter 10 outlines the destruction of the house of Ahab. Chapter 11 provides the story of Athaliah, the only female who reigned as a ruler in Judah. Joram's legacy is recorded in 2 Kings 8:18: "He walked in the way of the kings of Israel, as did the house of Ahab: for the daughter of Ahab was his wife: and he did evil in the sight of the Lord." At the death of her son Ahaziah, Athaliah proceeds to kill his sons—her rivals to the throne. But Jehosheba, the daughter of King Jehoram and sister of Ahaziah, rescues Joash, son of Ahaziah, and keeps him hidden in the temple for six years while Athaliah rules Judah (11:1–3). Athaliah's ruthlessness is not surprising when we recall that she is the daughter of Ahab and Jezebel and a worshiper of Baal. As is the case with many of the other rulers, Athaliah does evil in the eyes of the Lord. Like her mother before her, she is killed outside of the temple and not even provided a decent burial. "And they laid hands on her; and she went the way by the which the horses came into the king's house: and there was she slain" (v. 16). "And all the people of the land rejoiced, and the city was in quiet: and they slew Athaliah with the sword beside the king's house. Seven years old was Jehoash when he began to reign" (vv. 20–21).

The divided kingdom, a backsliding people, kings who continue the practice of evil and women who demand justice and interpret God's written Word complete the chronicles of the monarchy. In a world that has gone completely mad, two women engage in cannibalism, eating the son of one of the women. "And as the king of Israel was passing upon the wall, there cried a woman unto him, saying, Help my lord, O king. And he said, If the Lord do not help thee, whence shall I help thee?" (6:26–27). Instead of the wisdom of King Solomon, sought by two mothers in need of justice, the king can offer no help. This incident shows the dire consequences of a series of kings who "did evil in the eyes of the Lord" and led the divided nation into further chaos.

2 KINGS 22

When King Josiah turns eight years old, he becomes king over Judah. "His mother's name was Jedidah, the daughter of Adaiah of Boscath. And he did what was right in the sight of the Lord, and walked in all the ways of David his father" (22:1–2). In the eighteenth year of his reign the Book of the Law is found as the temple is prepared for reconstruction. Hilkiah, the high priest and Shaphan, the secretary to the king, makes the discovery. When they report their findings to the king, he reacts with repentance. "He rent his clothes. And the king commanded Hilkiah the priest, and Ahikam the son of Shaphan, and Achbor the son of Michaiah, and Shaphan the scribe, and Asahiah a servant of the king's, saying. Go ye, enquire of the Lord for me, and for the people, and for all Judah, concerning the words of this book that is found" (vv. 11–13).

This empowered and powerful entourage goes straight to Huldah, a keeper of the wardrobes and a woman obviously known as "of the Lord." "Though many of the Hebrews were given to idolatry and were ignorant of God, still the lamp of divine truth was kept burning in the heart of a woman named Huldah. She possessed two great qualities, righteousness and prophetic insight.... This prophetic power, never trusted to the undeserving was given to her because she loved God with all her heart" (All of the Women of the Bible, 1955). To this entourage, Huldah foretells with boldness and accuracy the doom of a people who stand and hear the written Word of God, declare they will do God's will, and yet return to doing evil in the eyes of the Lord! As with all the prophets of God, she begins her interpretation with the words, "Thus saith the Lord God of Israel" (2 Kin. 22:15).

> ***God of prophets,*** *priests, and kings, You have called me to carry Your Word with boldness and clarity to the world in which I live and serve. Give me a greater heart to love You, a greater mind to envision the future and a greater spirit to declare Your truth to all people!*

1ST CHRONICLES LIFE LESSONS

1 CHRONICLES 1–9

Chapters 1–9 list the people of God beginning with Adam. The story of Roots has reinforced for us the importance of knowing where you descended from and who your people were! In 1 Chronicles, there is no separating out the good, the bad, the pious, and the unrighteous. Their deeds are told and recounted. There are no "ideal" families. The people of God were birthed forth in full humanness. Their roles and assignments are listed that we might know the contributions they made to the overall history. They continue to show us that God uses the great and the small.

Potential Giver, thanks for showing us the worth of each individual in Your overall plan.

1 CHRONICLES 10–29

Chapters 10–29 detail how Saul takes his own life and David becomes king over Israel. Stories that detail the rise of a mighty king who conquers enemies like the Philistines and the household David establishes with wives and concubines are included. His bringing the ark of the covenant back to Jerusalem, writing songs of thanksgiving, making vows before God, and praying in humbleness over God's choice of him as king allow us to see God at work in a life. David's many victories, his plans for constructing the house of the Lord and the people who served him are detailed. The book concludes with Solomon's being acknowledged as king. David "died in a good old age, full of days, riches, and honour" (29:26).

> ***Prospering Sovereign,*** *thank You for choosing one who didn't look like, act like, or think of himself as "king material." Despite his appearance You looked at his heart and found him worthy! There is hope for me!*

2ND CHRONICLES LIFE LESSONS

2 CHRONICLES 1–9

Solomon asks for wisdom and prepares to build the temple. Its furnishings are detailed and the ark is brought and put in place. The dedication takes place. "When Solomon had made an end of praying, the fire came down from heaven, and consumed the burnt offering and the sacrifices; and the glory of the Lord filled the house. And the priests could not enter into the house of the Lord, because the glory of the Lord had filled the Lord's house" (7:1–3)

Amazing Presence, let Your glory fill this place!

2 CHRONICLES 10–36

The rise of the line of Judaic kings is detailed, including the reign of Athaliah, the queen mother who ruled for six years (22:12). Jerusalem falls in the last chapter of the book, and the people are carried into exile in Babylon. Cyrus, king of Persia, is moved by God to send the people back home for the rebuilding of the land seventy years later.

__Covenant-Remembering God,__ Your grace and mercy are astonishing.

EZRA
LIFE LESSONS

EZRA 1–2

Chapters one and two chronicle Cyrus, king of Persia, as a foreigner, Gentile, nonbeliever, outsider, and infidel! Yet it is recorded: "Now in the first year of Cyrus king of Persia, that the word of the Lord by the mouth of Jeremiah might be fulfilled, the Lord stirred up the spirit of Cyrus king of Persia, that he made a proclamation throughout all his kingdom, and put it also in writing, saying, Thus saith Cyrus king of

Persia, The Lord God of heaven hath given me all the kingdoms of the earth; and he hath charged me to build him an house at Jerusalem, which is in Judah. . . . And whosoever remaineth in any place where he sojourneth, let the men of his place help him with silver, and with gold, and with goods, and with beasts, beside the freewill offering for the house of God that is in Jerusalem" (1:1–4).

Again, it is made perfectly clear that God will use anyone and anything to fulfill His purpose. When the people of God decide to worship idols, God raises up an "idol worshiper" with a mind to build a temple in Jerusalem! What Israel is unable to accomplish will be accomplish at the hand of a foreign king. The whole earth belongs to God! God gets the glory and the temple despite who "thinks" they own it. In the same manner that the portable tabernacle in the wilderness was to be furnished by the "freewill offerings" that the Israelites collected from the Egyptians before the Exodus, once again the people are to bring the Lord an offering. God may not look like, act like, or be like what you expect. God will come disguised in "foreigners." Zerubbabel, a priest, began the work (3:8–9) and worship was restored. "So that the people could not discern the noise of the shout of joy from the noise of the weeping people: for the people shouted with a loud shout, and the noise was heard afar off" (v. 13).

> ***Supplier of Every Need,*** *help me to remember that my needs may be supplied by what is "foreign" to me. Any way You choose to bless me, let me receive it with gratitude.*

EZRA 7-10

Despite opposition from diverse "ruling" factions and delays, the temple is rebuilt and dedicated. Ezra is "a ready scribe in the law of Moses, which the Lord God of Israel had given" (7:6). The king had granted him everything he asked, for the hand of the Lord was upon him. Ezra had devoted himself to the study and observance of the Law of the Lord, and to teaching its decrees and laws in Israel (vv. 1–10). And God speaks to Ezra about intermarriage: "The people of Israel, and the priests, and the Levites, have not separated themselves from the people of the lands, doing according to their abominations... they have taken of their daughters for themselves, and for their sons: so that the hold seed have mingled themselves with the people of those lands: yea, the hand of the princes and rulers hath chief in this trespass" (9:1–2). The people confess their sin: "We have trespassed against out God, and have taken strange wives of the people of the land: yet now there is hope in Israel concerning this thing'" (10:2). "Then the congregation answered and said with a loud voice, As thou hast said, so must we do.... Let now our rulers of all the congregation stand, and let them which have taken strange wives in our cities come at appointed times... until the fierce wrath of our God for this matter be turned from us" (vv. 12–15). The Book of Ezra ends with a listing of all of the "guilty" parties.

Holy One, help me to remain alert and caring of those in the world around me. Keep me sensitive to those who have not yet come into the knowledge of You. And keep me separate from them in the ways I think and behave, so that I might influence them with my love for You.

NEHEMIAH LIFE LESSONS

NEHEMIAH 1–5

Chapters 1–2 outline the process of Nehemiah's preparation to rebuild the wall of Jerusalem. Chapters 3–5 show the building process and the opposition to that process. "They said unto me, The remnant that are left of the captivity there in the province are in great affliction and reproach: the wall of Jerusalem also is broken down, and the gates thereof are burned with fire. And it came to pass, when I heard these words, that I sat down and wept'" (1:3–4). Nehemiah had a good job in the palace as the king's cupbearer. Yet he was distressed about the conditions of his homeland. His employer, King Artaxerxes, sent him to Jerusalem as the newly appointed governor to rebuild the city's walls. Faced with opposition and delay as he inspects the wall, Nehemiah declares to several of his critics: "The God of heaven, he will prosper us; therefore we his servants will arise and build: but ye have not portion, nor right, nor memorial, in Jerusalem" (2:19–20).

Rebuilder of Torn and Burned Places, when others are working and I can't join in the labor, assist me with keeping my mouth shut so that I don't forfeit my share in Your generous rewards.

NEHEMIAH 6–13

The wall is completed (6:15). The doors to the gates are set in place. The gatekeepers, singers, and Levites are appointed. Guards are posted. "Now the city was large and great: but the people were few therein, and the houses were not builded. And my God put into mine heart to gather together the nobles, and the rulers, and the people, that they might be reckoned by genealogy of them which came up at the first, and found written therein" (7:4–5). "Upon the first day of the seventh month. And he read therein before the street that was before the water gate from the morning until midday, before the men and women, and those that could understand; and the ears of all the people were attentive unto the book of the law. . . . And all the people answered, Amen, Amen, with lifting up their hands: and they bowed their heads, and worshipped the Lord with their faces to the ground" (8:2–6). The people join in fasting, prayer and confession of their sin. In chapter nine, a signed agreement to keep the Law is enabled.

In chapter 10, the city of Jerusalem is repopulated. In chapter 11, the wall is dedicated. In chapters 12 and 13, new reforms by Ezra and Nehemiah are established.

Remember me, O my God, for good (Neh. 13:31).

ESTHER LIFE LESSONS

ESTHER 1

Vashti refuses to be viewed as an object for her husband, Xerxes. When she embarrasses him after he orders her to parade before his drunken associates, he has this reaction: "Therefore was the king very wroth, and his anger burned in him" (1:12). In consultation with his "wise men, which knew the times, (for so was the king's manner toward all that knew law and judgment" (v. 13). One spoke the truth: "Vashti the queen hath not done wrong to the king only, but also to all the princes, and to all the people that are in all the provinces of the king . . . Likewise shall the ladies of Persia and Media say this day unto all the king's princes, which have heard of the deed of the queen. Thus shall there arise too much contempt and wrath. If it please the king, let there go a royal commandment from him . . . that Vashti come no more before king Ahasuerus; and let the king give her royal estate unto another that is better than she'" (vv. 16, 18–19).

Vashti's refusal sets the stage for a drunken group of "little boys" to become upset that their personal "kingdoms" may come tumbling down around their feet if their wives behave in this insulting and unseemly manner. Her name is to be stricken from the royal records as if she never existed! Yet, her refusal opens the way for God to move on behalf of the Israelites, who are living in exile without voice or land. Once again, God chooses to allow a foreigner—a woman—to be a vessel for bringing about deliverance as part of a greater plan.

> **Divine Planner,** *people come and go from the stage of life. Just allow me to play my role, with quiet strength and dignity.*

ESTHER 2

"Let there be fair young virgins sought for the king: And let the king appoint officers in all the provinces of his kingdom, that they may gather together all the fair young virgins unto Shushan the palace, to the house of the women, unto the custody of Hege the king's chamberlain, keeper of women; and let their things for purification be given to them: And let the maiden which pleaseth the king be queen instead of Vashti. And the thing pleased the king; and he did so'" (2:2–4). The search for a new queen begins. We meet Mordecai and his ward, Hadassah, both of whom are exiles from Jerusalem, and Mordecai has his own plans for Hadassah, whose Persian name is Esther. "He brought up Hadassah, that is, Esther, his uncle's daughter: for she had neither father nor mother, and the maid was fair and beautiful; whom Mordecai, when her rather and mother were dead, took for his own daughter" (v. 7). Esther is taken with other young women to the palace. She does not reveal her nationality, because Mordecai warns her not to do so. ".Mordecai walked every day before the court of the women's house, to know how Esther did, and what should become of her" (v. 11). A twelve-month beauty regimen is required for her training (v. 12). Then the young women are turned over to the eunuch in charge of the concubines (v. 14). Esther wins the favor of all (v. 15). Since she pleases the king, she become his queen (v. 17). Meanwhile, while Mordecai sits at the king's gates, he discovers a plot to kill the king. He reports the plot to Esther, who tells the king (vv. 21–23).

God who sees inward beauty, let me win favor in Your sight.

ESTHER 3–4

In chapter three, we meet Haman, a descendent of Agag, the king of the Amalekites, the most bitter enemy of the Jews. Haman is promoted higher than all the other nobles. Everyone kneels down to pay him homage with the exception of Mordecai. "When Haman saw that Mordecai bowed not, nor did him reverence, then was Haman full of wrath. And he thought scorn to lay hands on Mordecai alone; for they had shewed him the people of Mordecai: wherefore

Haman sought to destroy all the Jews that were throughout the whole kingdom of Ahasuerus, even the people of Mordecai" (3:5). Haman reveals took his plot to the king who gives it his stamp of approval. "Do with them as it seemeth good to thee" (v. 11). This is an attempt at ethnic cleansing at its ultimate advantage. But, God provides their way of escape with Esther. In chapter four, Mordecai proceeds to remind Esther of her ethnic identity. "Think not with thyself that thou shalt escape in the king's house, more than all the Jews. For if thou altogether holdest thy peace at this time, then shall there enlargement and deliverance arise to the Jews from another place; but thou and thy father's house shall be destroyed: and who knoweth whether thou are come to the kingdom for such a time as this?"" (4:13–14). Esther calls for a national fast among the Jews. She makes her declaration to go and see the king even though it may cause her to lose her life.

> ***Bodacious God,*** *the righteous are as bold as a lion. Let my roar be heard where needed today.*

ESTHER 5

Knowing that Xerxes is an emotional man and not a rational thinker, Esther resorts to the old adage, "The way to a mans heart is through his stomach." She prepares a meal and invites both the king and Haman to attend. They come as she bids. While she's planning a meal, Haman is instructed by his wife, Zeresh, and all of his friends: "Let a gallows be made of fifty cubits high, and to morrow speak thou unto the king that Mordecai may be hanged thereon: then go thou in merrily with the king unto the banquet. And the thing pleased Haman; and he caused the gallows to be made" (5:14).

> ***Great God,*** *I hear You say, "When you dig a ditch, dig two. One for Your enemy; the other one for You!" Help me not to dig ditches!*

ESTHER 6–9

A restless king gets up in the night and has the Book of Chronicles read to him. He decides to honor Mordecai. He asks Haman how to honor a worthy man. Haman thinks of himself as the worthy man and suggests a parade of pomp and circumstance. The king agrees. The God of irony has the king instruct Haman to parade Mordecai through the town! As Haman is lamenting this sad state of affairs, the eunuchs come to hurry him to Queen Esther's feast. At the feast, she tells the king of the plight of her people, the Jews. "Then Haman was afraid before the king and queen. And the king rising from the banquet of wine in his wrath went into the palace garden" (7:6–7). While the king is out, Haman throws himself on the mercy of Queen Esther, pleading for his life. The king reenters the room and accuses Haman of the attempted sexual assault of his queen. Haman later is hanged on the gallows he had prepared for Mordecai (vv. 8–10). The king makes this decree: "Behold, I have given Esther the house of Haman, and him they have hanged upon the gallows, because he laid his hand upon the Jews" (8:7). That decree is followed by another one: "The king granted the Jews which were in every city to gather themselves together, and to stand for their life, . . . And many of the people of the land became Jews; for the fear of the Jews fell upon them" (vv. 11, 17). The Jews are victorious. The holy day of Purim is instituted to signify this national day of rejoicing. It is an edict of the queen! (9:32).

JOB
LIFE LESSONS

JOB 1

Job exercised concern for his family. Experience demonstrates that once a parent, always a parent. Parents naturally provide for and nurture their children. Parents of adult children pray for and counsel as they have opportunity.

> *Parent of Parents, give me the wisdom to be the parent I need to be for my underage or grown children, as well as for those in my community.*

Because of Job's great wealth and abundant blessing, Satan questions Job's motivations. God permits Job to be tested. God is keenly aware of our every human situation, and does permit testing. The tests are for our refinement as well as for the glory of God, who helps us to go through them and come out victoriously! When his wife comes to challenge his suffering, Job maintains that he has done no wrong.

> *Helper of the Helpless, when I am tested, please help me to draw close to You for strength and wisdom.*

Job acknowledges the sovereignty of God when the bottom had fallen out of everything important to him. He says, "The Lord gave, and the Lord hath taken away; blessed be the name of the Lord" (1:21). Praising God when things are going well is commendable, but having the ability to offer praise when everything goes wrong is a sign of genuine maturity and trust.

> *Sovereign God, help me to praise You when things are going well and when they are not.*

JOB 2–19

The friends and associates of Job come to "grieve" with him. They come with the common social understanding that Job has either sinned against God or has so contemplated sin until these tests are a warning. They urge Job to "fess up" and allow a contrite spirit to relieve him of this present distress. Job maintains his integrity. In the face of social pressure, Job lays his experience against community wisdom and norms. In the midst of painful suffering and the loss of all his relatives and friends, Job clings to his personal conviction that God would ultimately not disappoint him. He said, "I know that my redeemer liveth, and that he shall stand at the latter day upon the earth" (19:25–27).

> *Faithful Friend,* when I am experiencing painful suffering and no one seems to understand, help me to know that You will never leave me, and that ultimately I will see Your hand in the midst of the most desperate situation and be filled with wisdom, which will lead me to unending joy.

JOB 23

Job, in the midst of his suffering, seeks God. He wants and needs answers as to why this situation is happening to him. He knows the hurt of feeling forsaken. Yet he also knows that faith need not falter in such desperate times. He testifies of having sought for God in every known direction. Despite the seeming fruitlessness of his search, Job remains confident that "[God] knoweth the way that I take: when he hath tried me, I shall come forth as gold" (23:10).

> *Testing God,* in those times when I feel abandoned and alone, help me to know that You are still with me. Teach me not to doubt Your absence in times of testing.

JOB 38–41

God answers Job out of the whirlwind. Through His questions God reveals perfect knowledge, infinite wisdom, and vast immensity. God's questions help Job begins to understand His justice, love for creation, and absolute power. Job now knows that God is more than sufficient for all human needs. Faith in God's power and love are what sustains believers today through good times and bad.

> *Questioning God, help me to comprehend more about Your sufficiency. The story of Job helps me to better understand that You not only care for me, but that You care enough never to leave me nor forsake me.*

JOB 42

Job repents. "I know that thou canst do every thing, . . . Wherefore I abhor myself, and repent in dust and ashes" (42:2–6). The end of the story is better than the beginning. "The Lord blessed the latter end of Job more than his beginning" (v. 12). The family fortune is restored. Mrs. Job births seven additional sons, but their names are not recorded. However, three beautiful daughters are born: Jemima, Kezia, and Keren-happuch. "In all the land were no women found so fair as the daughters of Job: and their father gave them inheritance among their brethren" (vv. 14–15). This is mighty good news!

> *Dear God, I repent, as Job did, of my sins. Let me enjoy Your blessing again.*

PSALM LIFE LESSONS

PSALM 1

Psalm 1 describes two types of people: the "blessed" person is one who orders his or her life according to the Word of God ("law of the Lord," v. 2). Such a person is stable, fruitful, enduring, and prosperous. In contrast, the "ungodly" person is unstable, unfruitful, and unprotected from certain judgment.

> *Blessing God, help me to find delight in Your word so that I will always choose the path that leads to the fulfilled, fruitful life in You. Help me to avoid the ungodly path that leads to a lack of fruitfulness, as well as judgment from You.*

PSALM 8

Psalm 8 refers to the honor God has bestowed on us. We can know, feel, and act in ways similar to God's ways because we are made us in that divine image, the Imago Dei. How marvelous is the God whose love, wisdom, and power were breathed into us "in the beginning!"

> *Creative Creator, I praise You for the honor You have bestowed on me in making me in Your image and likeness.*

PSALM 16

Psalm 16 expresses the author's appreciation for the ability to enjoy a personal and intimate relationship with God. God is acknowledged as all sovereign and all sufficient (v. 5–6). The Psalm also expresses God's counsel (v. 7), God faithfulness (vv. 8–10), and ends with the affirmation of eternal joy at God's right hand—a never-ending relationship (vv. 9–11).

> ***Inviting God,*** *like the author, I also praise You for Your willingness to indwell those who believe in You, and for the blessings You provide both here and hereafter.*

PSALM 18

In Psalm 18, David praises God for deliverance from Saul. His expressions, while reflective of his own unique culture and circumstances, reveal truths about God, which are applicable anytime: God is a secure place to stand in times of stress ("a rock," v. 2); God hears our calls for help (v. 6); God is faithful (v. 25); God turns our "gloom into light" (v. 28); and God's Word is flawless and therefore totally reliable (v. 30). David testifies that only God can enable us to maneuver through the most harrowing of circumstances (v. 33).

> ***Delivering God,*** *You have revealed such awesome truths in Your Living Word. Help me to appropriate these truths for my life so that I can function each day in ways that honor You, bless others, and satisfy me.*

PSALM 23

In Psalm 23, David praises the Lord—who has been his shepherd—for sufficiency, rest, and refreshment (v. 2); restoration and guidance (v. 3); protection and discipline (v. 4); fellowship and honor (v. 5); and goodness and mercy both here on earth and in heaven forever.

> ***Shepherding God,*** *I thank You and praise You for Your sufficiency and comfort for me.*

PSALM 27

Psalm 27 expresses the psalmist's confidence that the Lord will give him victory over those who desire to do him evil. Because the Lord (and no one else) is his "light" (v. 1) and the source of his well-being, whom should he fear? He has evaluated the essentials of life and has decided that "dwelling in the house of the Lord" (v. 4) and seeking God (v. 8) are at the top of his list! His delight in the Lord moves him to encourage others to do as he did: "Wait on the Lord" (v. 14), a concept which means to eagerly anticipate that God will do what is necessary.

> ***God Who Comes,*** *in light of Your provision for my well-being, help me to always give You all of my affection. Help me to trust You for the wisdom and strength to do the right thing, knowing that to "wait" does not always mean to be idle, but to be expectant, with total dependence on the wisdom and strength that You provide.*

PSALM 37

In Psalm 37, David shares some lessons he has learned from walking with God: If you "trust in the Lord and do good" you will "dwell in the land" (v. 3). If you delight yourself in the Lord, the Lord will grant the desires of your heart (v. 4). If you commit your way unto God, your righteousness will shine (v. 6). If you don't run ahead of the Lord ("Be still and know" (Ps. 46:10)), you will inherit the land (vv. 7–9). If the Lord delights in you, God will make your steps firm and will keep you from falling (v. 24).

> *Attentive God, You are teaching me some valuable lessons about Yourself. Help me to be responsive to Your teaching and to order my steps according to Your Word.*

PSALM 42–43

The psalmist encourages others to "hope thou in God" (42:5, 11; 43:5). For Christian believers, hope is more than wishful anticipation that things will somehow get better. Because of our relationship with God who is all-sufficient for all our needs, our hope is certain because it is anchored in the One who cannot fail.

> *Hope of the World, I praise You for the hope You offer to those who place their trust in You. When I am tempted to be discouraged, please remind me that I need not be because You have promised*

victory for those whose confidence is in You. You are absolutely trustworthy.

PSALM 51

Psalm 51 is the prayer of repentance and confession which David prayed after the man of God, Nathan, comes and points out that "you are the man" who has taken advantage of Uriah's "one little ewe lamb!" David prays for mercy because of God's unfailing love (v. 1). He asks for his sins to be blotted out, his soul cleansed (v. 2). Then David confesses to knowing his own sin. He understands God's right judgment against him (v. 4). Then David helps us to comprehend that evil was implanted in us due to the original sin of our first parents, Adam and Eve (v. 5). And David begs of wisdom (v. 6). Restoration and joy are sought (v. 8). David asks for a pure heart and a steadfast spirit (v. 10). The appeal for God's Holy Spirit (the anointing) not to be taken from him is clear (v. 11). To be sustained by a spirit willing to do the right thing is voiced (v. 12). Then David promises to testify on God's behalf and to teach others to turn back to God after sin is committed (v. 13).

***Restoring Redeemer,** help me always to confess my sin and turn to You for healing, restoration, and forgiveness.*

PSALM 87

Psalm 87:4 lists five nations that will be gathered to worship the Lord in Zion: Rahab, Babylon, Philistia, Tyre, and Cush. Each of these nations sprang from Ham (Gen. 10:6–10), and shows God's glorious plans for these people of color. These texts demonstrate that while people of African descent are often rejected or ignored in our day, such treatment does not represent the love and plan of God, who accepts people of every nation who love and obey Him (see Acts 10:34–35).

> ***Inclusive God,*** *thank You for Your love for all people. Thank You for Your wonderful and inclusive plan to include people of African descent among the diverse groups that You will gather in Zion.*

PSALM 118

Psalm 118:8 is the exact center of the Bible! "It is better to trust in the Lord than to put confidence in man." "Who" you trust and "where" you seek refuge are the essential components of all religions. As women, it is good for us to be reminded that no human male can be our ultimate source. There is only one God! The Psalm's focus is on our having confidence in God's eternal, unchanging love. Regardless of the situations we face, this gives us both hope and confidence.

Trusting Refuge, "I shall not die, but live and declare the works of my Lord" (v. 17).

PSALM 139

In Psalm 139, David praises God for His omniscience, omnipresence, and omnipotence. God's knowledge is expressed in verses 1–6; God's omnipresence in verses 7–12; God's omnipotence, love, and providence in verses 13–18.

All-Seeing, All-Knowing, All-Powerful and Everywhere Present God, You are keenly aware of all that concerns me. When I am tempted to feel lonely, powerless, and abandoned, please remind me of who You are and what I mean to You.

PSALM 150

Psalm 150 is a closing hymn of praise. All of creation offers praise. Every musical instrument is tuned in praise to the Magnificent Creator. The worship of God resounds in every sphere of the universe. The anonymous writer of this hymn declares, "Let every thing that hath breath praise the Lord. Praise ye the Lord!" (150:6).

Praiseworthy God, all the universe exalts You. From the dry sprouting desert to the bubbling singing waters; from the grand and lofty mountains to the small oak budding in the forest; from the aged planets to the newly "found" galaxy—all of creation praises only You. As they respond to Your voice thundering, even in the silence of the longest night, I add my tiny voice and offer You my humble praise!

PROVERBS LIFE LESSON

PROVERBS 1

Proverbs 1:1–7 sets forth the purpose of the book which, among other objectives, is to impart wisdom, justice, judgment, and equity. These attributes should be the objectives of every person, especially those who claim identification with God. The author declares that in pursuit of these character traits the starting place is the "fear of the Lord" (v. 7). Since the Lord is wise, just, and impartial, our seeking to emulate these qualities will cause us to become "followers of God, as dear children" (Eph. 5:1).

__Original One,__ help my striving to be more like You.

PROVERBS 3

Proverbs 3:5–6 has been referred to many times because it contains principles for discovering the will of God. Someone observed that 90 percent of ascertaining the will of God is having the desire to obey it once we know it. Someone else observed that these verses express action on the part of two parties: God and us. God's part is to direct our paths. Our part is to trust and not lean on our own understanding (v. 5). As long as we are doing our part we need not become stressed out wondering what God will do. God is a promise keeper!

> ***Promise Keeper,*** *deepen my will to follow where You lead.*

PROVERBS 18

Proverbs 18:16 makes reference to the person who knows, develops, and operates in her or his spiritual gifts: "A man's gift maketh room for him, and bringeth him before great men." Neither people nor situations can block what God has in store for us if we are faithful in doing what God has given us to do. Spiritual gifts come from God alone. When we operate within our area of giftedness, God opens the doors and takes us to places and people we could never imagine! The key is knowing your gift.

> ***Gift Giver,*** *stir within me the ability to walk in the area You have outlined through my spiritual gift.*

PROVERBS 18

Proverbs 18:21 informs us that "death and life are in the power of the tongue." We get what we say! We create our worlds with our words. Since we are made in the Imago Dei (the divine image of God) who spoke the world into existence, we have the same creative powers. It is in our best interest to watch our words!

> ***Wisdom of the Ages,*** *guard my tongue and keep my life.*

PROVERBS 22

Proverbs 22:1 indicates that a good name is preferable to great riches, and loving favor is preferred to silver and gold. One's character (what a person is when no one is looking) and reputation are of greater value than material treasures. That is because God is the ultimate Judge of our destiny and will look beyond our outward trappings to examine our hearts. Money has little value, especially when the owner has such low character as to be untrustworthy and uncaring.

> ***Examiner of Hearts,*** *grant me favor and a good name which honors You.*

PROVERBS 22

Proverbs 22:6 exhorts parents to "train up a child in the way he should go: and when he is old, he will not depart from it." This proverb expresses results which are generally true, attested to by the many upright children who have been nurtured by godly parents. Experience demonstrates, however, that despite godly parents' efforts at "training…in the way they should go," a child may reject that training and go astray. In such cases, the Bible is not proved unreliable. The nature of proverbs is that they frequently express general truths—not absolute reality.

> ***Ultimate Parent,*** *I'm so glad that mothers and fathers I did not even know prayed for me to return to Your divine path.*

PROVERBS 29

Proverbs 29:15 refutes the teachings of Dr. Spock! "The rod and reproof give wisdom: but a child left to himself bringeth his mother to shame." Here discipline is encouraged. Discipline is not abuse; it is love in action for the correction of wrong behavior. Because God loves us, we too are disciplined. Modern society has tried to steer us away from this course of action. All we have to do is look around us to see where this folly has brought us!

> ***Strong Discipliner,*** *both Your rod and Your staff comfort me.*

PROVERBS 31

In Proverbs 31:10–31, a strong mother speaks to her son and describes the "virtuous" king and his selection of a "virtuous" woman. She is characterized by hard work, planning, and godly living—all for the benefit of her husband, children, and community. Her godly character is highlighted as the secret of her success (v. 30). The man who marries her knows that he has an invaluable prize!

> ***Eternal God,*** *help me to be the woman You would have me to be.*

ECCLESIASTES LIFE LESSONS

ECCLESIASTES 1–2

The author describes his search for meaning in human affairs and concludes that all is "vanity and vexation of spirit" (2:11). He declares the monotony of nature and the impossibility of anything new: "The thing that hath been, it is that which shall be; and that which is done is that which shall be done: and there is no new thing under the sun" (1:9). He then admits to discovering what many people do not have, that "things" (status, wealth, possessions, and so on) cannot satisfy the deepest longings of the human heart. Though expressed differently, the African theologian, Augustine, came to the same conclusion: "Our souls are restless until we find our rest in God." Despite these knowledgeable observations, we continue the insatiable search for meaning in things. There is no question that physical needs are important; the error is in the imbalance of allowing materialism to outstrip the spiritual.

> ***Satisfying Portion,** help me to keep the proper balance between the material and the spiritual. Help me to know that it is my relationship with You that enables me to keep all things in proper perspective.*

ECCLESIASTES 3

In chapter 3, the author expresses the belief that there is a time for everything and that these times are ordered by God who "hath made every thing beautiful in his time" (v. 11). The study in contrast is made simple by valuing the organization of our time. For there is time for everything and there are seasons for every purpose. Knowing how to discern the "time" and the "season" requires the wisdom of God. There is a "season" for nurturing others. There also is a time for nurturing oneself.

> ***Unchanging God,** teach me how to wisely manage my gift of time and seasons.*

ECCLESIASTES 5

Ecclesiastes 5:18 declares that "it is good... to enjoy the good of all his labour that he taketh under the sun all the days of his life, which God giveth him." Making good choices is crucial to living a well-ordered and God-approved life. Therefore, it is essential that we gain a purpose for our lives. Living to our fullest potential is a requirement for a satisfying life. Just working to make money to survive does not bring satisfaction. To live fully requires that we discover our God-given purpose so that we can do what we love and allow the monetary benefits to follow!

> ***Satisfier of the Longing Heart,*** *let the very center of my being explode with my divine purpose breathed into me at my "beginning."*

ECCLESIASTES 9–12

Ecclesiastes 12:13 gives the grand conclusion: "Fear God"! Life boils down to our personal relationship with the Creator of heaven and earth. What we amass in life will only grant temporary satisfaction. Regardless of how many "things" we acquire, how many people we supervise, how many mansions we build or how many obstacles we jump over in this life, there is only one chief requirement for eternal life and that is to keep the reverence of God as our first priority. We are to enjoy life such as it is, but focus on eternity. Since we cannot predict the future (9:1; 11:5–6) and only in this life can work be done, we are advised, "Whatsoever thy hand findeth to do, do it with thy might" (9:10). Wise people recognize the brevity of life (Ps. 90:10–12) and the critical nature of it. They establish worthwhile and God-approved goals and order their lives accordingly.

Heart's Desire, *keep my eyes focused on You!*

SONG OF SOLOMON LIFE LESSONS

SONG OF SOLOMON 1

The attraction between a male and female is natural and stated openly by a woman to her beloved (Song 1:1–4). There is a longing for sexual fulfillment. And, there is the warning that such attraction should not result in intimacy, until marriage has been consummated. In recent years, this clearly stated command by God that sexual activity should only occur within the bounds of marriage (Ex. 20:14) has been violated. The consequences have been disastrous: guilt, unwanted children, child abuse, and abortion, with its subsequent depression and guilt.

SONG OF SOLOMON 2

"I am sick with love" (2:5) reflects a deepening of the woman's affection for her lover. This growth of love points to the courtship that takes place between the two. Courtship should be a time when two lovers investigate their suitability for each other. Are they compatible for each other (which is not the same as sexual experimentation, which is clearly forbidden by the Bible)? Although accepted by contemporary social mores, exploited by movie and television themes, and virtually unheard of within the church, sex outside of marriage is expressly forbidden in Scripture (see Ex. 20:14). The scare of the sexually transmitted AIDS epidemic has caused media to take up the cry: "When you sleep with one, you sleep with all with whom that person has previously slept." It has been scientifically and medically documented, that there is no such thing as "safe sex." Any sex outside of marriage is sin.

> **God,** *giver of sexuality and self-control, keep me within your boundaries.*

SONG OF SOLOMON 3–4

The wedding scene details how the lover, most likely Solomon, prepared for the wedding with an expensive chariot (3:9) in which to meet his bride (4:9). He describes her beauty and his deep love for her in anticipation of the ceremony (4:1–17). Changes in culture may result in different formats for weddings, but the basic principle of lovers covenanting in the presence of witnesses to be loyal to each other need not change. For believers in Jesus Christ, that commitment ought to also be facilitated by a minister of the gospel. Additionally, our society requires the couple to obtain a marriage license in order to regulate the state's interest in married couples. The growing practice of persons simply living together without adhering to these fundamental principles violates biblical teaching.

> *O God,* keep me like "a garden inclosed" until I covenant with a man in marriage (4:12).

SONG OF SOLOMON 5-6

The lovers are always making quick departures and hasty escapes. They continually want to get alone to deepen their relationship with each other. Weems suggests that this couple may have been in an interracial, interethnic marriage which would not have been sanctioned by the "town" (WBC). Hence, the constant appeals to the "daughters of Jerusalem" as she seeks her beloved. As a married couple now (5:2–6:9), the wife describes the distance that has developed between herself and her husband either emotionally or literally (5:2–7). She senses the strained relationship and takes steps to strengthen it. In return, the husband reaffirms his love for his wife (6:3–9). Just as this relationship needed to be strengthened, so all marriage relationships need to be guarded. When distance develops between couples, steps need to be taken to renew it.

Dear God, strengthen my relationship with my husband. "I am my beloved's and my beloved is mine" (6:3).

SONG OF SOLOMON 6–8

The husband and wife celebrate each other's desirable traits (6:10–8:4). He celebrates her charm (7:1–9); she expresses her longing for him (8:1–4) as they become more intimate. Marriage permits ultimate intimacy between lovers. Such closeness points to and illustrates the abiding relationship believers can have with God through Jesus Christ. "I am my beloved's, and his desire is towards me" (7:10). This woman has come into her own. She has decided, "my vineyard, which is mine, is before me" to give (8:12). "The Song of Songs advocates balance in female and male relationships, urging mutuality, not domination; interdependence, not enmity" (WBC, 160).

Garden Giver, help me to plant, nurture, weed, grow, and harvest in my own yard.

ISAIAH LIFE LESSONS

ISAIAH 1–6

Isaiah 1:1–6:13 sets the stage for the work of the prophet. We are introduced to him and immediately hear the accusations of God against Israel. "Hear, O heavens, and give ear, O earth: for the Lord hath spoken, I have nourished and brought up children, and they have rebelled against me. The ox knoweth his owner, and the ass his master's crib: but Israel doth not know, my people doth not consider'" (1:1–4). "How is the faithful city become an harlot! it was full of judgment; righteousness lodged in it; but now murderers" (v. 21). The great God of love, mercy, and justice has a severe complaint against these "children" who have walked away from the covenant.

It is easy to see how the imagery of a "woman gone bad" moves from a woman in particular to all of Israel as a whole. This is a forerunner of the common description of the church as "woman" and "bride of Christ." As the "spouse of the church," God is faithful to the covenant, providing and protecting as required by the vows of a covenantal relationship. However, the "wife," who is dependent, has "walked away," looking for another "lover." Judgment is pronounced upon Jerusalem and Judah.

We find several references to the roles of women in the rituals of the community. The roles of music making and lamenting are described in "The Song of the Vineyard" (chap. 5), and in the prophecy of 3:26, "Her gates shall lament and mourn; and she being desolate shall sit upon the ground." Even today, the role of "official" mourner belongs to the Jewish woman. Lamentations continue to be expressed through wailing and sitting on the ground, and an inability to dance or be lighthearted.

Tear Catcher, I am fulfilling my lamenting mission for Your people.

ISAIAH 7–9

Isaiah is clear about the time of his call to ministry: "In the year that king Uzziah died I saw also the Lord ... also I heard the voice of the Lord saying, Whom shall I send, and who will go for us? Then I said, Here am I; send me'" (6:1, 8). One of his first assignments is to warn King Ahaz, as powerful enemies threaten: "If ye will not believe, surely ye shall not be established" (7: 9). Ahaz is encouraged to keep the faith, for the coming of Immanuel is foretold (v. 14).

Every enemy is told to "associate yourselves, O ye people, and ye shall be broken in pieces; ... Take counsel together, and it shall come to nought; speak the word, and it shall not stand: for God is with us" (8:9–10). Yet Israel refuses to repent and return to God. Assyria will be raised up to get their attention. "And they shall look unto the earth; and behold trouble and darkness, dimness of anguish; and they shall be driven to darkness. Nevertheless the dimness shall not be such . . . For unto us a child is born, unto us a son is given: and the government shall be upon his shoulder: and his name shall be called Wonderful, Counselor, The mighty God, The everlasting Father, The Prince of Peace. Of the increase of his government and peace there shall be no" (8:22–9:1, 6–7).

Wonderful Counselor, Mighty and Everlasting God, Prince of Peace, worthy is Your name!

ISAIAH 12–39

Jesus is called "a rod out of the stem of Jesse . . . a root of Jesse, which shall stand for an ensign of the people; to it shall the Gentiles seek: and his rest shall be glorious" (11:1, 10). Songs of praise for God's salvation are proclaimed in chapter 12. Then there is a series of woes against Israel's enemies intermingled with songs of praise for God's mercy throughout chapters 12–35.

When King Hezekiah reminds God of his walking in righteousness, deliverance is promised: "I have heard thy prayer, I have seen thy tears: behold, I will add unto thy days fifteen years. And I will deliver thee and this city out of the hand of the king of Assyria: and I will defend this city" (38:5–6). Thank God for a king who did "that which was right in the sight of the Lord" (2 Chron. 29:2) and stood as an intercessor for his people!

Watching Savior, let my life be a witness of Your deliverance.

ISAIAH 40

Chapter 40 has a change of tenor. "Comfort ye, comfort ye my people, saith your God. Speak ye comfortably to Jerusalem, and cry unto her, that her warfare is accomplished, that her iniquity is pardoned: for she hath received of the Lord's hand double for all her sins. The voice of him that crieth in the wilderness, Prepare ye the way of the Lord, make straight in the desert a highway for our God. Every valley shall be exalted, and every mountain and hill shall be made low: and the crooked shall be made straight, and the rough places plain: And the glory of the Lord shall be revealed, and all flesh shall see it together: for the mouth of the Lord hath spoken it" (vv. 1–6).

Helper of Israel, thank You for goodness and mercy at work on our behalf.

JEREMIAH LIFE LESSONS

JEREMIAH 1

In chapter one, Jeremiah begins with the introduction of his call and his resistance. God declares, "Before I formed thee in the belly I knew thee; and before thou camest forth out of the womb I sanctified thee, and I ordained thee a prophet unto the nations" (v. 5).

Then God gives this charge: "See, I have this day set thee over the nations and over the kingdoms, to root out, and to pull down, and to destroy, and to throw down, to build, and to plant" (v. 10). "Thou therefore gird up thy loins, and arise, and speak unto them all that I command thee: be not dismayed at their faces, lest I confound thee before them … [T]hey shall fight against thee; but they shall not prevail against thee; for I am with thee" (vv. 17–19).

Immanuel, You were with me in my forming and calling. Speak Your instructions to me again.

JEREMIAH 30–52

The remaining chapters up to chapter 45 concern themselves with failed leadership as prophets deceive the people with words of peace. A lying priest imprisons Jeremiah

(20:1–6). Suffering and weeping occur as "Rachel [weeps] for her children" (31:15). We get a glimpse of hope threading its way through chapters 30–33. Healing and new life are promised and Jeremiah urges the people to believe that God will remove the yoke of bondage from their necks (30:8–9). Women will dance and laughter will be heard (31:13–14). Beginning with chapter 46, a message of destruction is proclaimed to the nations—a "day of the Lord's vengeance" for Israel's foes. The fall of Jerusalem is set as the last chapter—chapter 52-proclaims, "Thus Judah was carried away captive out of his own land" (v. 27).

__Righteous Judge of Every Nation,__ help me remain true to You!

LAMENTATIONS LIFE LESSONS

LAMENTATIONS 2

Chapter two finds the voice of the daughter of Zion lifted in outrage as she shouts in outrage at God for killing the people of the city, lamenting, "The Lord hath swallowed up all the habitations of Jacob, and hath not pitied" (v. 1). How like the hearts of many inner city mothers who have lost children to what is termed "urban violence" does "she" sound! The daughter of Zion's prayer may help contemporary women in their prayer. "Her" voice evokes the pain of women who have lost their children, who know sexual abuse, or who are victims of war and famine. To pray with the daughter of Zion is to join with the struggles of women around the globe. It is to reject victimhood by embracing the anger that can provide energy to transform relationships. It is to pour out "thine heart like water before the face of the Lord" (v. 19).

> ***God of My Heart,*** *You know the pain of my soul, for You watched Your own child die.*

LAMENTATIONS 3

Chapter three is spoken in the voice of a man. "I am the man that hath seen affliction" (v. 1). It is thought to be the wounded heart and spirit of Jeremiah. For 19 verses, he laments. Then there is a theological shift as he reflects on God's goodness in the past. "It is of the Lord's mercies that we are not consumed, because his compassions fail not. They are new every morning: great is thy faithfulness" (vv. 22–23). Hope is born!

> ***Hope of the World,*** *thank You for the tiny sparks of radiance that emerges in spite of the situations in which we find ourselves.*

LAMENTATIONS 4

Chapter four contrasts the former Jerusalem to its present misery. The plight of children seems to be a current concern: "The tongue of the sucking child cleaveth to the roof of his mouth for thirst: the young children ask bread, and no man breaketh it unto them. They that did feed delicately are desolate in the streets: they that were brought up in scarlet embrace dunghills" (vv. 4–5). Jeremiah leaves us with a vivid description of the fate of a people who have wandered far from their relationship with God. It was the sin of the people that had brought about their own destruction.

> **Bread of Heaven,** *feed me till I want no more.*

LAMENTATIONS 5

Chapter five lifts up Jeremiah's prayer to God for mercy. The people join in a prayer for restoration and favor from God. "Remember, O Lord, what is come upon us: consider, and behold our reproach" (v. 1). The verses go on to describe the devastation (vv. 2–11). "By praying with her, women may be able to give voice to their pain and despair, and, by voicing it, by expressing their anger, they may be able to move beyond circumstances of impasse" (WBC, 181). May women be able to announce with the daughter of Zion "Turn thou us unto thee, O Lord, and we shall be turned; renew our days as of old" (5:21).

> **O Restorer,** *renew me and restore me, so that I may serve You.*

EZEKIEL LIFE LESSONS

EZEKIEL 1–3

With the opening of Ezekiel's message, we are immediately caught up in his visions. "This was the appearance of the likeness of the glory of the Lord. And when I saw it, I fell upon my face, and I heard a voice of one that spake.... Son of man, stand upon thy feet and I will speak unto" (1:28–2:1). Ezekiel then details his call and God's instructions: "Be not afraid of them, neither be afraid of their words ... thou dost dwell among scorpions ... thou shalt speak my words unto them, whether they will hear, or whether they will forbear ... But thou, son of man, hear what I say unto thee; Be not thou rebellious ... eat that I give thee" (2:6–8). Ezekiel eats the scroll, which fills him and tastes "as honey for sweetness" (3:3).

> ***You Who Are Sweeter than Honey in the Honeycomb,*** *fill my mouth with Your words.*

EZEKIEL 4–24

Chapters 4–24 provide us with the symbolic messages. Ezekiel is called to "show" the unrepentant, exiled people their sin and God's just activities because of the rebellion of their hearts. First, he lies on his left side to symbolize the captivity of Israel; then he lies on his right side to symbolize God's judgment against Judah (4:4–9). "Wherefore, as I live, saith the Lord God; Surely, because thou hast defiled my sanctuary with all thy detestable things, and with all thine abominations, therefore will I also diminish thee; neither shall mine eye spare, neither will I have any pity. A third part of thee shall die with the pestilence, and with famine shall they be consumed in the midst of thee: and a their part shall fall by the sword round about thee; and I will scatter a third part into all the winds, and I will draw out a sword after them" (5:11–12). This is the punishment Israel and Judah have "earned" due to disobedience and failure to live up to their covenant with God.

In a vision Ezekiel sees the destruction of the temple at Jerusalem because of idol worship. There is judgment on Israel's lying, unjust leaders. False prophets are singled out for punishment and those who practice idol worship are condemned. Jerusalem is pictured as a useless vine (chap. 15) and an unfaithful woman (chap. 16). The overall curse of the entire nation is broken! "Behold, all souls are mine... the soul that sinneth, it shall die" (18:4).

The "professional" mourners are called again to "take thou up a lamentation for the princes of Israel, And say, What is thy mother? A lioness: she lay down among the lions... his voice should no more be heard upon the mountains of Israel" (19:1–2). In chapter 23, the analogy of Aholah and Aholibah is used to represent the whoredom of Samaria and Jerusalem who are both handed over to the Assyrians.

"Thus will I cause lewdness to cease out of the land, that all women may be taught not to do after your lewdness. And they shall recompense your lewdness upon you, an dye shall bear the sins of your idols: and ye shall know that I am the Lord God" (vv. 48–49).

Strong Deliverer, save us from ourselves!

EZEKIEL 25–37

Ezekiel pronounces judgment against a series of foreign nations in the laments of chapters 25–32. In chapter 33, we hear God speak again to Ezekiel. "So thou, O son of man, I have set thee a watchman unto the house of Israel; therefore thou shalt hear the word at my mouth, and warn them from me" (v. 7).

Chapter 34 is a prophecy against the shepherds of Israel who are concerned only about their own welfare. "Behold, I am against the shepherds; and I will require my flock at their hand, and cause them to cease from feeding the flock; neither shall the shepherds feed themselves any more; for I will deliver my flock from their mouth, that they may not be meat for them" (v. 10). Chapter 37 is one of the most well known passages, describing the valley of the dry bones that are restored to life with the Spirit of the Living God.

Breath of Life, breathe on me, fill me with Your Holy Spirit that I might live fully.

EZEKIEL 39-48

The message of Ezekiel closes with a series of visions. "In the five and twentieth year of our captivity, in the beginning of the year . . . behold a wall on the outside of the house round about" (40:1, 5). It is the hope of restoration. It is the promise of God. "Now will I bring again the captivity of Jacob, and have mercy upon the whole house of Israel, and will be jealous for my holy name. . .. Then shall they know that I am the Lord their God, which caused them to be led into captivity among the heathen: but I have gathered them unto their own land, and have left none of them anymore there. Neither will I hide my face any more from them: for I have poured out my spirit upon the house of Israel, saith the Lord God" (39:25–29).

DANIEL LIFE LESSONS

DANIEL 1-3

The first three chapters are teaching texts about loyalty. "And the king spake unto Ashpenaz the master of his eunuchs, that he should bring certain of the children of Israel, and of the king's seed, and of the princes; children in whom was no blemish, but well favoured, and skilful in all wisdom and cunning in knowledge, and understanding science, and such as had ability in them to stand in the king's palace, and whom they might teach the learning and the tongue of the Chaldeans.... But Daniel purposed in his heart that he would not defile himself with the portion of the king's meat, nor with the wine he drank: therefore he requested of the prince of the eunuchs that he might not defile himself" (1:3–4, 8).

The enemy wants to find "the cream of the crop" and make them assimilate, take off their identity and become "one of the crowd." God has commanded that we be different, that we be role models set apart to show God's glory wherever we happen to be—even in slavery or exile!

When Nebuchadnezzar made a golden image and demanded that everyone bow down and worship it, Shadrach, Meshach, and Abednego respond, "O Nebuchadnezzar, we are not careful to answer thee in this matter. If it be so, our God whom we serve is able to deliver us from the burning fiery furnace, and he will deliver us out of thine hand, O king. But if not, be it known unto thee, O king, that we will not serve thy gods, nor worship the golden image which thou hast set up" (3:16–18).

> ***O God,*** *help me pass the test of loyalty by remaining steadfast in my faith expression in this foreign land.*

DANIEL 2–5

Three of the chapters display God's wisdom at work through them. In chapter 2, Daniel interprets the king's dream about the crumbling of a metal statue: "Then the king made Daniel a great man, and gave him many great gifts. . . . Then Daniel requested of the king and he set Shadrach, Meshach, and Abednego, over the affairs of the province of Babylon: but Daniel sat in the gate of the king" (2:48–49). King Nebuchadnezzar dreamed of a big tree which was cut down and stripped bare. Daniel interpreted the dream, and challenged political power: "O, King, let my counsel be acceptable unto thee, and break off thy sins by righteousness, and thine iniquities by shewing mercy to the poor; if it may be a lengthening of thy tranquillity"(4:27). And the dream was fulfilled

In chapter five, King Belshazzar gave a great drinking party, using the goblets from God's holy temple. "In that same hour came forth fingers of a man's hand, and wrote over against the plaister of the wall. . . . And this is the writing that was written, MENE, MENE, TEKEL,UPHARSIN" (5:5, 25). Daniel gave the interpretation: "MENE; God hath numbered thy kingdom, and finished it. TEKEL; Thou art weighed in the balances, and art found wanting. PERES; Thy kingdom is divided, and given to the Medes and the Persians. Then commanded Belshazzar, and they clothed Daniel with scarlet, and put a chain of gold about his neck, and made a proclamation concerning him, that he should be the third ruler in the kingdom" (vv. 26–29). It pays to heed God's wisdom and to speak it when necessary, even to those who consider themselves to be "power"! We know who has the ultimate power!

> ***Power of the Powerless,*** *empower me to do what You command, wherever, whenever and to whomever!*

DANIEL 6–12

One of the most fascinating portion of the stories is the apocalypse or end-time revelation, that Daniel receives. Daniel is approached by an angelic being who details how God is already at work, intervening in history to destroy evil. Enemies plot against Daniel to stop his practice of praying three times daily to his God. The conspiracy works and Daniel is forced into a den of lions as a consequence. God intervenes and delivers (chap. 6). Then Daniel has a series of visions.

"When I, even I Daniel, had seen the vision, and sought for the meaning, then, behold, there stood before me as the appearance of a man. And I heard a man's voice … which called, and said, Gabriel, make this man to understand the vision.… He said unto me, Understand, O son of man: for at the time of the end shall be the vision.… And I Daniel fainted, and was sick certain days; afterward I rose up, and did the king's business; and I was astonished at the vision, but none understood" (7:1, 15; 8:17, 27). Daniel continued to receive revelations and to interpret them. He is promised at the end of the book, "Go thou thy way till the end be: for thou shalt rest, and stand in thy lot at the end of the days" (12:13). That is a great reward for loyalty and wisdom. Perhaps it's worth telling Jesus that it's all right to change your name!

Revealer of Hidden Things, thank You for trusting us with Your wisdom.

HOSEA LIFE LESSONS

HOSEA 1–3

Chapters 1–3 illustrate Hosea's call to marry Gomer, an unfaithful wife. She bears a son. God instructs Hosea to name the child, Jezreel, indicating the coming punishment for Israel in the valley of Jezreel (1:1–4). Gomer's second child is a daughter. God instructs Hosea to name her Lo-ruhamah, meaning, "I will no more have mercy on the house of Israel" (v. 6). After weaning this infant, Gomer conceives a third time and has another son. The child is named Lo-ammi, meaning "Ye are not my people, and I will not be your God" (v. 8). Gomer leaves home after this. "She shall follow after her lovers, but she shall not overtake them; and she shall seek them, but shall not find them" (2:7).

There is immediate sympathy for Hosea—a husband who has been done wrong! He symbolizes a brokenhearted God who has entered into covenant with Israel only to be rejected time after time. Yet there must be consideration of the pain of Gomer, constantly caught in adultery and loved despite her sin. Every mother can understand the guilt that lived inside. To leave your children in order to "seek other lovers" suggests a deep-seated, unexplainable pain which commentators have yet to uncover. Also there must be some consideration for the three children named to bear the guilt and shame of their mother's sin. The grand reality is that sin hurts all of us!

The covenant with Israel is dissolved because of unfaithful behavior on Israel's part. In chapter three, after Gomer's departure and shameful exposure to the world, God says to Hosea, "Go yet, love a woman beloved of her friend, yet an adulteress, according to the love of the Lord toward the children of Israel . . . So I bought her" (3:11–12). How wonderful it is for us to know that God still loves and is willing to redeem the person who sins.

> *Redeemer of Wanderers, how many times I've cheated on You! Forgive me. Cleanse me of my unfaithful ways. I want to be faithful to our covenant. I desire to be true to You.*

JOEL
LIFE LESSONS

JOEL 1

Chapter one opens with a plea to "ye old men, and give ear, all ye inhabitants of the land. Hath this been in your days, or even in the days of your fathers?" (1:2). The approaching enemy is compared to invading locusts. Joel wants to "wake up" his sleeping religious community and make them react to the severe consequences of their behavior in forgetting the covenant with Yahweh.

> ***To represent the grief of the people at the devastation of their country,*** *Joel invokes the image of a young woman mourning her husband in widow's weeds of sackcloth (v. 8). Joel's rallying cry is to "return wholeheartedly" to Yahweh (2:12). For Joel, repentance is no guarantee of deliverance. (WBC, 203–204)*

"Sanctify ye a fast, call a solemn assembly, gather the elders and all the inhabitants of the land into the house of the Lord your God . . . Alas for the day! for the day of the Lord is at hand, and as a destruction from the Almighty shall it come" (2:14–15).

> ***Zion's Deliverer,*** *hear our pleas. See our repentant hearts. Listen to our cry for mercy.*

JOEL 2

The Lord answers and takes pity on Zion (2:18). Material blessings of grain, new wine, and oil are promised (v. 19). Then three additional blessings are listed to be dispensed before the day of the Lord. There is the outpouring of the Holy Spirit upon all flesh (vv. 28–29). Cosmic signs are announced (vv. 30–31). Salvation is promised for Zion (v. 32). "Whereas in the past, the gift of prophecy was the prerogative of a few, in the future it will be an inclusive gift. Distinctions of age (old men and young men) gender (sons and daughters) social class (male and female servants) will be swept away in this common spiritual endowment." And everyone who calls on the name of the Lord shall be saved (WBC, 204; Joel 2:32).

Sweet Salvation, thank You for specifically including women in the Day of the Lord's outpouring!

AMOS LIFE LESSONS

AMOS 1–2

Chapters one and two are volatile warnings for repeated sins. There is judgment against Israel as God recounts their deliverance from Egypt, the prophets who led them, and the gift of the Promised Land. God's anger is clear. "Is it not even thus, O ye children of Israel? saith the Lord. But ye gave the Nazarites wine to drink; and commanded the prophets, saying, Prophesy not. Behold I am pressed under you, as a cart is pressed that is full of sheaves. Therefore the flight shall perish from the swift, and the strong shall not strengthen his force, neither shall the mighty deliver himself" (2:10–16). The Judge has called the court to order. There is no defense. Justice will be metered out and the punishment will be severe. The reasons for God's anger are pointed out with specificity: "They sold the righteous for silver, and the poor for a pair of shoes; That pant after the dust of the earth on the head of the poor, and turn aside the way of the meek: and a man and his father will go in unto the same maid, to profane my holy name . . . and they drink the wine of the condemned in the house of their god" (vv. 6–8). The people of Israel, from priest to commoner, have become unjust, uncaring, and unholy idol worshipers!

God of Grace and Mercy, help us!

AMOS 7

Chapter seven records Amos's visions of locusts, fire, and a plumbline. The first not to measure up to the straight, strict standards of the plumbline is Amaziah, the priest of Bethel. Amaziah sends words to King Jeroboam: "Amos hath conspired against thee in the midst of the house of Israel:

the land is not able to bear it" (7:10–11). Amos prophesies against Amaziah and his entire house for standing against the word of God. "Thy wife shall be an harlot in the city, and thy sons and thy daughters shall fall by the sword, and thy land shall be divided by" (7:17).

This is a socioeconomic curse that strips the priest of family and land, two items that have proven God's favor in the past. To signify that his wife would become a prostitute was the ultimate shame of a priest who was forbidden by the Leviticus holy codes to marry one. In this particular case, the women and the sons are "victims" of their father's sin. It is clear that the innocent suffer with the guilty when judgment is brought upon the land.

> ***Holy One,*** *help me to keep my focus on You and bring only honor to those of my house.*

AMOS 8

Chapter eight repeats the warnings of coming destruction, "They shall run to and fro . . . the fair virgins and young men faint for thirst . . . and, The manner of Beer-sheba liveth; even they shall fall, and never rise up again" (8:12–14). Chapter nine begins with the same tone of devastation, but there is a hint of God's grace: "I will destroy it off the face of the earth; saving that I will not utterly destroy the house of Jacob, saith the Lord" (9:8). Finally, Amos pronounces his benediction: God will "plant them upon their land, and they shall no more be pulled up out of their land which I have given them" (v. 15).

Consoler of the Condemned, we exalt Your extension of amazing grace!

OBADIAH LIFE LESSONS

OBADIAH 1

The pride of the Edomites resulted in God's judgment (v. 3). They thought that because their country was situated among the rocks, they were safe from all attacks by outside armies. Through Obadiah, God warns them that their high and lofty position would not prevent His judgment upon them (v. 4). We must be ever careful of pride. The surest antidote for pride is to always give the proper honor to the Lord. When God is in His proper place, our attitude will be one of humility. We see ourselves as God sees us.

Dear God, please help me to remember that pride always precedes a fall. Help me to give You Your rightful place in my life so that I will not fall victim to the sin of pride.

The Edomites rejoiced when Israel was judged, when the invaders carried off people and wealth (vv. 11–14). God shows His displeasure at such an arrogant attitude. We must be careful never to gloat over the misfortunes of others. Except for the grace of God, we could be in the same condition or worse.

> *Dear God,* *please help me never to look down on the misfortunes of others. Help me remember that instead of gloating over the misfortunes of others, I should instead seek to help them and be ever grateful for the mercy You have bestowed on me.*

Family feuds and sibling rivalry are not taken lightly by God. Competition and division are open invitations to danger and destruction. Arrogance and self-sufficiency smack against "family interdependence," which is modeled for the Christian church. We are an interlocked, dependent unit and God will not suffer us to be indifferent, harmful, or destructive toward each other. For women who have a tendency toward "petty jealousy" of each other, the warning is clear in verse 4: "thence will I bring thee down."

> *Architect of the Family,* *help me to be supportive, helpful, and loving to every sibling.*

JONAH LIFE LESSONS

JONAH 1

Chapter one details Jonah's running away from his assigned mission station. He gets others in trouble for his disobedience. The only thing left to do with the disobedient prophet comes from Jonah himself: "Take me up, and cast me forth into the sea.... I know that for my sake this great tempest is upon you" (1:11). The consequence was that "the Lord had prepared a great fish to swallow up Jonah. And Jonah was in the belly of the fish three days and three nights" (v. 17).

> *Miracle Working Wonder, is this a sign of Your gracious, loving compassion for us in Jesus Christ?*

JONAH 2

Chapter two finds Jonah praying in distress. God answers his prayer. "And the Lord spake unto the fish, and it vomited out Jonah upon the dry land" (2:10).

> *Answering God, in my distress I lift my voice of supplication to You.*

JONAH 3

Chapter three finds Jonah going to Nineveh, accomplishing his mission. "So Jonah arose, and went unto Nineveh, according to the word of the Lord" (3:3). He made a three-day journey in one day. As a result: "So the people of Nineveh believed God, and proclaimed a fast, and put on sackcloth, from the greatest of them even to the least of them" (v. 5). "And God saw their works, that they turned from their evil way; and God repented of the evil, that he had said that he would do unto them; and he did it not" (v. 10).

> ***Compassionate Heart,*** *thank You for Your grace and mercy!*

JONAH 4

"But it displeased Jonah exceedingly" (4:1). Jonah wants God to annihilate the Ninevites. It's the same attitude that an abused and violated woman would have about her abuser! Please take notice that Jonah makes no attempt to sound "nice" or "pious" or "holy." He is just plain mad! God allows Jonah his honest, human, and understandable anger. But, grace and mercy have already been dispatched!

> ***Gracious and Merciful Creator,*** *thank You for caring for even the worst of us. And, thank You for understanding the authentic feelings of my heart. Work in me in order to work through me to declare the unsearchable riches of Your love, even to those who have hurt me the most.*

MICAH LIFE LESSONS

MICAH 1–2

Chapters 1 and 2 describe the judgment that God will bring upon Jerusalem because of its incurable practice of sin. "Therefore I will make Samaria as an heap of the field … and all the graven images thereof shall be beaten to pieces, and all the hires thereof shall be burned with the fire, and all the idols thereof will I lay desolate: for she gathered it of the hire of an harlot, and they shall return to the hire of an" (1:6–7). The major charges of God against the people include the ways they perverted worship and their injustice toward the poor. Micah outlines the charges of God against city after city with bitter complaints and warnings of that which is to come as judgment. "Woe" is pronounced upon the false prophets who say, "They shall not prophesy to them, that they shall not take shame" (2:6). Even those whose responsibility is to care for the house of God have fallen into sin. They go so far as to make others feel comfortable with their sin! "The women of my people have ye cast out from their pleasant houses; from their children have ye taken away my glory forever" (v. 9).

Uncovering God, strip away my longing for only my personal comfort. Make me uncomfortable with the things You hate! I want Your blessing to rest, rule, and abide upon me and my house.

MICAH 3-4

Chapters three and four find Micah tearing away at the despicable deeds of the leaders and prophets. "Is it not for you to know judgment? Who hate the good, and love the evil; who pluck off their skin from off them, and their flesh from off their bones; Who also eat the flesh of my people, and flay their skin from off them; and they break their bones, and chop them in pieces, as for the pot, and as flesh within the caldron" (3:1–3). God hates ugly! When you decide to "do the wrong thing" which jeopardizes the small and insignificant in society, there is no out for you with God. God's anger is boiling and the declaration is made that "the seers be ashamed, and the diviners confounded; yea, they shall all cover their lips; for there is no answer of God" (v. 7). As with other prophets, the word of grace is extended: "In the last days . . . many nations shall come, and say, Come, and let us go up to the mountain of the Lord, and to the house of the God of Jacob'" (4:1–2). Micah's message is not all doom and gloom! There is always a way of repentance and forgiveness. God "hates" sin, yet loves sinners!

> ***Loving Creator,*** *thank You for being God and for providing the second, third, fourth, and fifth chance if needed for me to obey You!*

MICAH 5-7

Chapter five outlines the coming of the Messiah who will come from Bethlehem and be a shepherd, "in the strength of the Lord, in the majesty of the name of the Lord his God, ... this man shall be the peace" (5:4–5). Both the right living and the evildoers are given their destiny in this chapter. In chapter six, God sets a solid case against backsliding Israel: "He hath shewed thee, O man, what is good; and what doth the Lord require of thee, but to do justly, and to love mercy, and to walk humbly with thy God" (6:8). No excuse will be allowed, for the covenant and the Ten Commandments outline the way Israel is to behave and serve as role model for the rest of the world. Her misery is detailed in the chapter seven: "Woe is me! ... I will bear the indignation of the Lord, because I have sinned against him" (7:1, 9). Yet all is not lost. Micah waits in confidence that Israel will rise. "In the day that thy walls are to be built, in that day shall the decree be far removed" (v. 11). He concludes his message with a reminder to a loving and merciful God, "Thou wilt perform the truth to Jacob and the mercy to Abraham, which thou hast sworn unto our fathers from the days of old" (v. 20). God loved us enough to come in Jesus! That's what love means!

O Loving God, I confidently wait on You to act.

NAHUM LIFE LESSONS

NAHUM 1

Chapter one is clear and direct: "God is jealous, and the Lord revengeth; the Lord revengeth, and is furious; the Lord will take vengeance on his adversaries, and he reserveth wrath for his enemies. The Lord is slow to anger, and great in power, and will not at all acquit the wicked" (1:2–3). Judgment and punishment will come to those who mistreat God's people. This punishment may not come as soon as we would like it to, but God has promised that vengeance will occur. Our hands will be clean!

> *Avenging God,* thank You for relieving me of the responsibility to think of ways to "pay back" my enemies. Those who attack me also attack You. I leave them in Your hands.

NAHUM 2–3

Judgment is declared against the greatest, most fearsome enemy Israel had ever encountered. This chapter predicts the time when the Babylonians will come and destroy Nineveh. What they have done to both the northern and southern kingdoms of Israel is lightweight compared to what God has in mind for them. "Nineveh is of old like a pool of water: yet they shall flee away. Stand, stand, shall they cry; but none shall look back.... She is empty, and void, and waste: and the heart melteth, and the knees smite together, and much pain is in all loins, and the faces of them all gather blackness.... and the voice of they messengers shall no more be heard" (2:8, 10, 13).

Great rejoicing is heard and felt in Israel: "There is no healing of thy bruise; and thy would is grievous: all that hear the bruit of thee shall clap the hands over thee: for upon whom hath not thy wickedness passed continually?" (3:19). This is bad news for the enemy and good news for those God loved!

Wealth of the Nations, I run to You for refuge in frightening times, for You are a secure place of safety. Thank You for protection as well as comfort.

HABAKKUK LIFE LESSONS

HABAKKUK 1–2

Chapters one and two contain dialogue with the prophet framing some harsh and difficult questions for God. He wants to understand how the Creator of heaven and earth could tolerate the wickedness going on in Judah. Habakkuk is concerned about the violence that the people of Judah are doing to themselves by departing from the covenant relationship, as well as the violence that is sure to come in judgment. The sin within Judah is painful. "Why dost thou shew me iniquity, and cause me to behold grievance? for spoiling and violence are before me: and there are that rise up strife and contention. Therefore the law is slacked, and judgment doth never go forth: for the wicked doth compass about the righteous; therefore wrong judgment" (1:3-4). Standing at the top of the city wall, Habakkuk has the advantage of being able to "look down" and get a true view of what is going on both within and around the city where God is to reign. Sick and tired of being sick and tired, Habakkuk decides to have a little talk with his "companion." So he asks a series of questions. And, his "friend" speaks an answer. "I will work a work in your days, which ye will not believe, though it be told you. For lo, I raise up the Chaldeans" (vv. 5-6). Violence begets violence!

> ***Wall of Protection,*** *take away the spirit of violence. Help me to speak out against violence.*

HABAKKUK 1-2

Chapter one draws to a close with Habakkuk's second complaint. "Art thou not from everlasting, O Lord my God, mine Holy One? we shall not die, O Lord, thou hast ordained them for judgment; and O mighty God, thou hast established them for correction. Thou art of purer eyes than to behold evil, and canst not look on iniquity" (1:12–13). That's a good question for women to grapple with as the ravages of racism, sexism, and classism try to hem us in on every side! We all want an answer regarding God's timeframe of "getting" those who have done us wrong! This is when God instructs Habakkuk to "write the vision, and make it plain" (2:2). Payday is coming. Payback also is coming! The righteous must live out their days in faith. Evil will not triumph! "The Lord is in his holy temple: let all the earth keep silence before him" (v. 20).

***Rock of Ages,** cleft for me, let me hide myself in Thee!*

HABAKKUK 3

The book closes with Habakkuk's prayer of praise for God's faithfulness. The prophet had been told that Judah would pay the penalties for her sin and it would not be a pretty sight! But his questions are given answers. Like the psalms of David, the word Selah, which indicates a time of reflection and affirmation of the truth, appears. "O Lord, I have heard thy speech, and was afraid: O Lord, revive thy work in the midst of the years, in the midst of the years make known; in wrath remember mercy'" (3:2). We each have days and seasons when it seems that "evil" and the wicked have the upper hand. It can be difficult to "see" why God permits things and people to get so bad and to act so ugly! Habakkuk is seeing what's on the way. In full confidence of the God he serves and questions, Habakkuk includes these reassuring words for our "waiting" hearts.

Coming Savior, "Although the fig tree shall not blossom, neither shall fruit be in the vines; the labour of the olive shall fail, and the fields shall yield no meat; the flock shall be cut off from the fold, and there shall be no herd in the stalls: Yet I will rejoice in the Lord, I will joy in the God of my salvation. The Lord God is my strength . . . and he will make me to walk upon mine high places" (vv. 17–19).

ZEPHANIAH LIFE LESSONS

ZEPHANIAH 1

Chapter one rings out a severe warning of coming destruction aimed at Judah and those who lived in sight of the temple where the name of the Holy One of Israel was to be worshiped. Yet the people worship idols. "I will cut off the remnant of Baal from this place, and the name of the Chemarims with the priests; And them that worship the host of heaven upon the housetops; and them that worship and swear . . . by Malcham . . . and those that have not sought the

Lord, not enquired for him" (1:4–6). Idol worship is the first sin that God mentions in the Ten Commandments. Checking our horoscopes, calling "the psychic hotline," and going to visit those who can "read" your future are ways of participating in idolatry! The "starry host" is alive! When we put anything before God—a spouse or significant other, children, a job, the acquisition of wealth—we engage in the active practice of idols! Beware!

Creator of the sun, moon, and stars, help me know and practice true worship of You who holds my life and future within Your capable hands.

ZEPHANIAH 2–3

Chapter two commands the calling together of a sacred assembly. "Gather yourselves together, yea, gather together, O nation not desired; Before the decree bring forth . . . before the day of the Lord's anger come upon you. Seek ye the Lord" (2:1–3). A series of pronouncements against the "enemies" of the Lord is metered out. Chapter three begins to outline the future of Jerusalem when the destruction has occurred and restoration is provided. God promises: "In that day shalt thou not be ashamed for all thy doings . . . I will also leave in the midst of thee an afflicted and poor people, and they shall trust in the name of the Lord. The remnant of Israel shall not do iniquity, not speak lies, neither shall a deceitful tongue be found in their mouth . . . Sing, O daughter of" (3:8–14).

Keeper of the Remnant, work meekness and humility within me. I want to be ready when You come! My heart sings and rejoices in Your saving grace.

HAGGAI LIFE LESSONS

HAGGAI 1

Chapter one begins with the people's excuse for not completing the work assigned them by God. "The time if not come, the time that the Lord's house should be built'"" (1:2). Their own priorities took precedent over God, who had delivered them once again. Happy to be "home," but caught in great community tension, the people decided that God's house could wait! Coming "home" was not a picnic. Those who had been displaced by foreign occupation and those who had been taken into captivity were at odds over who owned what land, house, or well. Property issues consumed much of their time and caused much community infighting. These social tensions were set against too little rain, poor crop cultivation, and a rate of inflation that rendered them unable to return to "business as usual." Things were tough and not getting any better. They were "doing the best they could" to get their personal houses in order and trying to survive. God's house was put off as a project "on the back burner." God says through Haggai, "Consider your ways. Ye have sown much, and bring in little; ye ear, but ye have not enough; ye drink, but ye are not filled with drink; ye clothe you, but there is none warm; and he that earneth wages earneth wages to put it into a bag with holes.... Ye looked for much, and, lo it came to little; and when ye brought it home, I did blow upon it. Why? saith the Lord of hosts. Because of mine house that is waste, and ye run every man unto his won house, Therefore the heaven over you is stayed from dew, and the earth is stayed from her fruit" (vv. 5–6, 9–11). The indictment against Israel is serious.

There is no mistake. They set their priorities wrongly. God works against them as fast as they work for themselves. They cannot win! Their labors are futile!

> *Harvest Giver, I work diligently to earn my daily bread. Yet I hear You say that when I remember to honor You first, You will provide all that I need. Help me to always establish You as the very first of my priorities! I don't want to work against my own blessings that You desire to send my way!*

HAGGAI 2

Chapter two contains the key verse for our prosperity and continued blessing. As the people begin work on God's house with renewed vigor and commitment, God speaks a word of encouragement. "Yet now be strong...be strong... be strong, all ye people of the land, saith the Lord, and work: for I am with you... According to the word that I covenanted with you . . . so my spirit remaineth among you: Fear ye not." The word of God to "Be strong" came to the leader, Zerubbabel, who had been appointed by the foreign King Darius to do the work of rebuilding. The word of God, "Be strong" came to the high priest, Joshua. The word of God, "Be strong" came also to all the people of the land. The reason behind their being able to do the work assigned and take care of their homes and families was due to the covenant God had made with them years ago. They were to simply "work"—do their part, follow instructions, and rely upon the provisions of an able God. Dannibelle Hall sang it best: "Little becomes much when you place it in the Master's hand." As the people return to work on God's house their blessing is promised again: "From this day will I bless you" (2:19). "[I] will make thee as a signet ring, for I have chosen thee" (v. 23).

Faithful Sovereign, all that I have belongs to You. I covenant to make You my first priority as I "work" on my physical temple and work in my local congregation to uplift Your glorious name.

ZECHARIAH LIFE LESSONS

ZECHARIAH 1-8

Chapter one is a repeat of Haggai's prophecy of God's anger over the ways of Israel that resulted in her exile. We are introduced again to a thread of hope in the midst of their return. ""I am returned to Jerusalem with mercies: my house shall be built in it, saith the Lord of hosts, and a line shall be stretched forth upon Jerusalem.... My cities through prosperity shall yet be spread abroad; and the Lord shall yet comfort Zion, and shall yet choose Jerusalem"" (1:16–17). Then we get a view of Zechariah's visions: messengers reporting to God all who have oppressed Judah; four horns representing the world powers who will be scattered; a man with a measuring line who declares that Jerusalem will be too small for all the people who will come to fill her walls; clean clothes for the priest which speak of garments of sin exchanged for garments of righteousness; a lampstand which has unlimited supply of oil foretelling the indwelling of the Holy Spirit in living souls; a flying scroll, which represents God's Word which will judge the world; a woman who represents the idol worshipers shipped back to Babylonia in a basket (which shows that sin is removed from Israel), and four horses and chariots who will execute God's world judgment. Chapter eight provides God's promise to bless Jerusalem and another call to the people not to stop the work. "Let your hands be strong... that the temple might be built.... fear not, but let your hands be strong'" (8:9, 13).

Temple Builder, work on this building, called me, so that it is worthy of carrying Your great name.

ZECHARIAH 9–14

Chapter nine foretells the coming of the Messiah after work on the temple is complete: "Rejoice greatly, O daughter of Zion; shout, O daughter of Jerusalem: behold, thy King cometh unto thee: he is just, and having salvation; lowly, and riding upon an ass... he shall speak peace unto the heathen; and his dominion shall be from sea even to sea, and from the river even to the ends of the earth" (9:9–10). The temple in Jerusalem is only a "dream" to signify the rule of Jesus Christ over the whole of God's people. "And men shall dwell in it, and there shall be no more utter destruction; but Jerusalem shall be safely inhabited" (14:11).

MALACHI LIFE LESSONS

MALACHI 1–3

Chapter one is a harsh denouncement of the priests who offer blemished sacrifices unto God. "Who is there even among you that would shut the doors for nought? neither do ye kindle fire on mine altar for nought, I have no pleasure in you, saith the Lord of hosts, neither will I accept an offering at your" (1:10). Chapter two continues with additional curses: "I will even send a curse upon you, and I will curse your blessings: yea, I have cursed them already, because ye do not lay it to heart" (2:2). Judah's unfaithfulness is set in the context of a marriage covenant being broken. "Judah hath dealt treacherously, and an abomination is committed in Israel and in Jerusalem; for Judah hath profaned the holiness of the Lord which he loved, and hath married the daughter of a strange god.... For the Lord, the God of Israel, saith that he hateth putting away'" (vv. 11, 16). Useless tears and empty words "have wearied the Lord" (v. 17). So God sends "my messenger and he shall prepare the way before me" (3:1).

"But who may abide the day of his coming? . . . he is like a refiner's fire, and like fullers' soap . . . And I will come near to you to judgment; and I will be a swift witness against the sorcerers, and against false swearers, and against those that oppress the hireling in his wages, the widow, and the fatherless, and that turn aside the stranger from his right, and fear not me, saith the Lord of hosts" (3:2–5).

Lord Almighty, purify me, cleanse me, and give me open ears to hear what You say to me, Your child.

MALACHI 3

The book draws to a close. The last words from God for this covenant people ends with a detailed explanation of tithing, a practice that is deliberately misunderstood today. As God gets ready to shut up the heavens, the "last word" is not about "pledges." It is not about tipping. It is not even about "stewardship Sundays." This "word" is about the way God's people were involved in robbing the One who was their source. How do we rob God? "In tithes and offerings. Ye are cursed with a curse: for ye have robbed me, even this whole nation. Bring ye all the tithes... prove me now herewith... if I will not open you the windows of heaven, and pour you out a blessing, that there shall not be room enough to receive it'" (3:8–12). The tithe is ten percent of whatever we receive as income or gain. The tithe belongs to God! The tithe comes off the top! The tithe is from gross income and not net, after taxes, Social Security, and so on have been removed! For all of what you have received, whether from a well-paying position or from the rolls of public aid, the tithe is a way that all of us can be equal in our giving unto the Lord!

Generous God, You have given me all! Prepare my heart to return unto You the tithe of my resources, my time, and my gifts. It's the least I can do!

MALACHI 4

Because God is compassionate and loving, the promise of grace and mercy is found within this last book: "But unto you that fear my name shall the Sun of righteousness arise with healing in his wings; and ye shall go forth, and grow up as calves of the stall" (4:2).

***Thanks be** unto a merciful God!*

NEW TESTAMENT
LIFE
LESSONS

From the Bible

MATTHEW LIFE LESSONS

MATTHEW 1

Matthew includes four women besides Mary in his genealogy of Jesus: Tamar, Rahab, Ruth, and Uriah's wife Bathsheba. This shows the inclusive attitude of Matthew toward women. Tamar and Rahab were Canaanites, Ruth was a Moabite, Bathsheba's husband Uriah was a Hittite. All of this reflects the grace of God in implementing His plan of redemption. It leads us to the conclusion that just as God has demonstrated His grace in the past, so He continues to do so in the present age. He is a God of grace and is available to each one who calls on Him in sincerity and truth.

Dear God, I praise You for Your unchanging grace. Help me to claim Your grace for my daily needs. Amen.

MATTHEW 4

In the account of Jesus' temptation by Satan (Matt. 4:1–11), we notice how the tempter appealed to the fundamental drives of human nature, hunger, self-protection, and desire for power—the same areas where Satan tempts us. Notice also that Jesus resisted the temptation through His appeal to God's Word, "It is written…" Our knowledge of and confidence in the written Word of God will be critical when we are faced with Satan's temptations.

> ***Dear God,*** *when I am tempted by Satan, help me to rely on Your word to resist. May Your Holy Spirit give me strength to say "No" to his attacks. Amen.*

MATTHEW 6

The prayer our Lord taught His disciples (Matt. 6:9–13) is a pattern for our prayers. The priority should be as follows: acknowledging and affirming God as the sovereign one whose name should be elevated and hallowed, praying that His will should prevail on earth as it is in heaven; praying for our daily needs, for forgiveness, and for deliverance form Satan, the evil one. Keeping the priority as Jesus outlined in this prayer will keep us focused properly.

> ***Dear God,*** *Thank You for providing this model for our prayers. Help me always to give You and Your will top priority when I pray. Amen.*

MATTHEW 9

As Jesus went about teaching, preaching, and healing people, He was deeply moved by their condition. He saw them as harassed and helpless like sheep without a shepherd. We as His followers should be moved as He was.

Dear God, please help me to see people as Jesus saw them. Give me the desire and ability to help someone along life's highway so You will be pleased. Amen.

MATTHEW 14

Jesus was concerned about the masses of people who had remained with Him all day to hear the Word of God and were now hungry (Matt. 14:15–21). He took the five loaves and two fish—all that was available—and gave thanks. Rather than complain that He had only five loaves and two fish, He thanked God for what He did have. This reminds us that when we take whatever we have and place it (money, abilities, and time) in the hands of Jesus, He can take our little and multiply it to satisfy the needs of others.

Dear God, I give you what I have. I pray that you would multiply it.

MATTHEW 27

We are told that many women were at the cross, having come from Galilee to use their resources to care for Jesus. Their devotion to our Lord is remarkable. When many of the disciples fled, these women were still there watching from a distance, agonizing over the suffering of their Master, whom they knew was innocent. Through the years, women have repeated acts such as these as they have agonized over the suffering of the innocent, using their resources to relieve the hurting.

> *Dear God,* may I, like these women, continue the tradition of serving those who are hurting, knowing that You do not overlook the least cup of water given in Your name Amen.

MARK LIFE LESSONS

MARK 1

Mark tells us that Jesus went out to pray while it was still dark (Mark 1:35). Jesus maintained a practice of communing with God. He knew the value of worship and communication with His heavenly Father. Doubtlessly from this fellowship with God He derived strength and direction for accomplishing His mission here on earth.

> *Dear God,* teach me to spend time with You in prayer and meditation, knowing that from such times I will gain emotional, spiritual, and physical strength to accomplish Your purpose for my life. Amen.

MARK 2

Jesus' healing of the paralytic (2:1–12) teaches us that Jesus can both heal and forgive sins. 1 John 1:9 tells us, "If we confess our sins, he is faithful and just to forgive us our sins and to cleanse us from all unrighteousness."

> *Dear Jesus, when I fail You, please give me the grace to confess my sins so I can experience the joy of Your forgiveness. Amen.*

MARK 2

Jesus challenged the Pharisees to place the needy people above their traditions. He did so by refusing to condemn His disciples for plucking grain on the Sabbath and also by healing a man with a shriveled hand on the Sabbath (Mark 2:23–3:5). We should not allow our traditions to prevent us from helping those who are in need.

> *Dear God, please give me wisdom to never allow traditions to stand in the way of my helping others who are in need. Amen.*

MARK 4

Jesus calmed the raging sea, then asked the disciples, "Why are ye so fearful? How is it that ye have no faith?" (Mark 4:40). Is that not the same question Jesus would ask us when we are faced with great turmoil in life? The antidote for fear is trust in a loving God. Certainly the cares of life often test our faith and cause us to fear. In those moments we can call on God and anticipate peace and calmness in our inner selves. Learning to trust is a growing process, but a rewarding one.

> ***Dear Storm-calming God,*** *when the cares of this life overwhelm me, please remind me to come to You for solace and peace. Amen.*

MARK 5

Jesus healed the demon-possessed man (Mark 5:1–20). Mark portrays this man as desperate, helpless, and hopeless—until Jesus came! "Sitting, clothed, and in his right mind" (v. 15) describes how completely Jesus had changed his condition. No person is beyond the reach of God's power.

> ***Dear God,*** *help me to know that no situation is beyond Your power to overcome. Help me to trust You in my most difficult situations, and when in Your wisdom You delay an answer, give me the grace to wait on You. Amen.*

Jesus raised a dead girl (Mark 5:21–24, 35–42). Jairus, the synagogue ruler, came with a request for Jesus to heal his daughter. When she died, the messengers concluded it was useless for Jesus to come to the man's house. The mourners made fun of Jesus' statement that the damsel was asleep. Jesus proceeded because He knew what none of them knew—His power over death. Not only does this incident give us encouragement for trusting Jesus' power in this life, it lets us know that He can raise us at the appropriate time.

> *Dear God, I praise You for Your unlimited power. Please remind me of Your power when I'm tempted to believe my situation is hopeless.*

A woman who had a very intimate feminine problem discovered that just by touching the hem of Jesus' garment, she was made whole. On the one hand her faith was very small, on the other it was very strong. Jesus said the faith of a mustard seed is all we need. The critical difference is not the amount of the faith but the Person in whom we trust.

> *Dear Great Physician, show me how to bring my most intimate concerns to You, knowing that it is not how much faith I have as it is that I have faith in You. Help me to know that You alone are the great Healer, and when You choose not to heal, You can give grace to help me endure what You permit to come into my experience Amen.*

We learn in Mark's Gospel, that Jesus is a healer! Jesus also healed a sick woman (5:25–34). This woman had been bleeding for 12 years, unable to get relief from the many physicians who attended her. Her faith in the power of Jesus' garment without His conscious attention is remarkable and resulted in total healing.

> *Dear Lord, help me to remember You can heal me both physically and emotionally.*

MARK 9

Jesus used a little child to teach His disciples the need for humility in serving Him (Mark 9:33–39). We often get caught up in the desire for power and recognition for what we do for Christ. On one occasion, Jesus taught that people who do things for recognition are at that very time receiving all the reward they will ever get (Matt. 6:2, 5). Only what we do for Christ will earn His "well done."

> *Dear God, teach me to serve You without expecting recognition from people. Amen.*

MARK 10

We also learn, in the Gospel of Mark that God knows what our true motives are. This is shown when the rich young ruler wanted to know what he needed to do to make sure of eternal life (Mark 10:17–31). Hearing him say he had kept all the commandments, Jesus sought to help this young man see that he really hadn't. He did not really love God with all his heart because he was not willing to sell his possessions and follow Jesus. His trust was really in his material possessions.

> *Dear God, please teach me to trust in You, not my possessions, knowing that if my trust is in You, I will not be devastated when material losses come.*

MARK 14

"Jesus said, Let her alone" (Mark 14:6). He was rebuking those who criticized the woman (Mary) who had anointed His head with expensive perfume (John 12:1–8). Jesus said Mary anointed Him to prepare His body for burial. Did Mary have insight into the destiny of Jesus that others apparently did not have? Jesus understood her motive when others did not.

> *Dear God,* Thank You for understanding my motives when others do not Give me grace to bear with those who may not understand my deepest emotions Amen.

MARK 16

Three women arrive at Jesus' tomb early in the morning to anoint His body properly. There had not been time to do so when He was buried. So, these women lovingly arose early on the first day of the week to show their care for Jesus. On their way to do what they regarded as proper, they were rewarded with being the first to learn that the tomb was empty. Often God reserves unexpected, special blessings for those who faithfully do the things they know are right.

> *Dear God,* May I faithfully do what You want me to do, knowing that You sometimes reserve blessings for those who faithfully serve You. Amen.

LUKE
LIFE LESSONS

LUKE 1

In the birth of John the Baptist (1:5–25), we learn many life lessons. The appearance of an angel to announce the birth of John, the Messiah's forerunner, was the fulfillment of prophecy made by the prophet Malachi (4:5). Luke shows the continuity of God's activity from the Old Testament into the New. We learn that God keeps His word. God kept His word in relationship to Abraham, Isaac, and Jacob, and this was repeated many times during the history of Israel.

Dear God, I praise You for Your faithfulness in always keeping Your word. May I never doubt Your promises to be faithful to me. Amen.

From the point where Jesus' birth is announced, we learn that God will use ordinary people to fulfill His promises (1:26–38). Jesus' birth is foretold. Mary's response to the angel's announcement was greeted with a resounding, "I am available to You, Lord" (paraphrased). God used her readiness to obey as the means of bringing salvation to the world. God still looks for people like Mary who are eager to be vessels for accomplishing His will.

Dear God, please grant me the willingness to be available to You for whatever Your will is for my life. Help me to believe that "where You guide You will provide." Amen.

We also learn important lessons from Mary's visit to Elisabeth and Mary's song (Luke 1:39–55). Certainly, the angel's announcement to Mary that she would give birth to Jesus was sufficient to assure her of the significance of her child's birth. But now Elisabeth gave her further confirmation. This elderly relative called Mary's child her "Lord" (Luke 1:43). Furthermore, Elisabeth seemed aware that Mary had a heavenly visitor appear even before Mary had told her. Sometimes God gives us more than one confirmation of His will.

Dear God, thank You for those times when You give me added confirmation that I am doing Your will. Amen.

JOHN
LIFE LESSONS

JOHN 1

John's purpose in writing was to show that Jesus Christ is from God, speaks for God, and is the only way of access to God. The prologue to his Gospel makes the identity of Christ quite clear. Christ was in the beginning with God, and was, in fact, God. He came to the earth to show us the way back to God. Every person in the world must come to grips with who Jesus is and decide whether to trust Him for life, or reject Him.

> ***Dear God,*** *please open my eyes to the truth of Your Son's identity. Help me to trust Him as my own personal Savior and life according to Your will and way. Amen.*

JOHN 4

Jesus challenged His disciples to lift their eyes to see the enormity of human need and accept the challenge of being workers who will help bring in the harvest.

> ***Dear God,*** *please open my eyes to see someone in need today. Give me the love and ability to help someone who needs Your love in a special way.*

JOHN 6

Five thousand men plus women and children were hungry, and Jesus fed them.

> ***Holy Provider,*** *thank You for attending to all my physical needs.*

ACTS LIFE LESSONS

ACTS 1–2

In Acts, Luke continues his detailed report to Theophilus by testifying about the acts of the Holy Spirit, who had been sent, as promised by Jesus on the day of His ascension. We find an historical narrative of the life, growth, and struggle in the early days of the church of Christ, which began on the day of Pentecost in Jerusalem and then spread abroad. The Gospel was spread because the Holy Spirit started working in the life of those believers who had waited in the upper room until they were empowered by a supernatural force. They were empowered to "run and tell" the wonderful story of Jesus Christ. Matthias was chosen to replace Judas, and "they all continued with one accord in prayer and supplication, with the women, and Mary the mother of Jesus" (Acts 1:14).

Peter became the chief spokesperson to a waiting crowd that sought an explanation of what had happened to the group of 120. As he drew his message to a close, he charged, "Therefore let all the house of Israel know assuredly, that God hath made that same Jesus, whom ye have crucified, both Lord and Christ. Now when they heard this, they were pricked in their heart, and said unto Peter and to the rest of the apostles, Men and brethren, what shall we do? Then

Peter said unto them, Repent, and be baptized every one of you in the name of Jesus Christ for the remission of sins... and the same day there were added unto them about three thousand souls... And the Lord added to the church daily such as should be saved" (2:36–38, 41, 47).

Life and Resurrection, thank You for Your saving grace that covers me.

ACTS 4–5

As the group of believers came together, there was a communal spirit where "neither said any of them that ought of the things which he possessed was his own, but they had all things" (Acts 4:32). However, the spirit of greed was present. Ananias and his wife Sapphira were the first two persons who tried to make a profit from withholding possessions, and lied about it. Both, on separate occasions, lied to the Holy Spirit (5:3 and 5:10). Both dropped dead, and "great fear came upon all the church, and upon as many as heard about these things" (Acts 5:11).

Spirit of Truth, rid me of the spirit of deceitfulness.

ACTS 6–9

As the numbers of believers increased, there was strife between cultures. "And in those days... there arose a mur-

muring of the Grecians against the Hebrews because their widows were neglected in the daily ministration [distribution of food]" (Acts 6:1). The role of "deacon" was arranged by the twelve apostles to care for the needs of the women. The church grew and persecution broke out against the church in Jerusalem, and "they were all scattered abroad throughout the regions of Judaea and Samaria, except the apostles" (Acts 8:1). Saul began an all-out campaign to destroy the church, "entering into every house, and haling men and women committed them to prison" (Acts 8:3). There was no respect of person there! Our sisters suffered for the spread of the "Realm of God." And, eventually Saul was apprehended by God (Acts 9:1–17). It is recorded, "Saul increased the more in strength, and confounded the Jews which dwelt at Damascus, proving that this is very Christ.... Then had the churches rest throughout all Judaea and Galilee and Samaria, and were edified, and walking in the fear of the Lord, and in the comfort of the Holy Ghost, were multiplied" (Acts 9:22, 31).

> ***God of Increase,*** *how I magnify Your name for coming to use one like me!*

ACTS 9

Peter traveled the area, preaching and healing. "Now there was at Joppa a certain disciple named Tabitha, which by interpretation is called Dorcas: this woman was full of good works and almsdeeds which she did" (Acts 9:36). Tabitha was the first and only woman specifically called a "disciple" in Scripture! Her "good works" for the widows in Joppa out of her own resources was well-known. She had not been commissioned, like the "deacons" in Jerusalem, but how often do women receive the same role value and public acclaim for the ministry they perform? It seemed to make little difference that her ministry was called "good works." What mattered was that "Peter . . . kneeled down, and prayed, and turning him to the body said, Tabitha, arise. And she opened her eyes: and when she saw Peter, she sat up. And he gave her his hand, and lifted her up, and when he had called the saints and widows, presented her alive. And it was known throughout all Joppa; and many believed in the Lord" (Acts 9:40–42).

> ***Power of Good Works,*** *sustain me in what You have called me to do in Your name.*

ACTS 12

Peter was arrested by Herod and kept in prison, bound with chains, and placed between two guards. "Peter therefore was kept in prison: but prayer was made without ceasing of the church unto God for him (Acts 12:5). When God sent an angel to answer their prayers and Peter showed up at the house of Mary the mother of John Mark, a servant named Rhoda answered the door, but didn't open it upon hearing Peter's voice. She ran back to inform the prayer group that Peter was at the door and they responded, "Thou art mad" (Acts 12:15).

As she kept insisting that it was Peter, but failed to let him into the house, they decided, "It is his angel" (Acts 12:15). Finally, the door was opened and Rhoda's announcement was seen to be true. It seems that regardless of the news that women bring, it must first be discounted. Usually, the authority of a woman's word is challenged and put to the test.

***Voice of the Unheard,** help me to keep making Your unbelievable announcements!*

ACTS 16

On a second missionary journey, God sent Paul and his companions to Philippi where a church was planted. "On the Sabbath we went out of the city by a river side, where prayer was wont to be made; and we sat down, and spake unto the women which resorted thither. And a certain woman named Lydia, a seller of purple [cloth], from the city of Thyatira, which worshipped God heard us" (Acts 16:13–15). These women constituted the initial church! They were already praying, in worship, and were ready to receive the news of Jesus Christ. It is interesting to note that they were at the river, at the water, at the source of refreshment where women have always gathered to share news. The men, "expected" to find a captive audience there! In 16:40 we read that Lydia's house becomes a "house church" and "[Paul and Silas] went out of prison, and entered into the house of Lydia: and when they had seen the brethren, they comforted them."

***Fountain of Life,** fall afresh upon me!*

ACTS 18

In Corinth, Paul met a clergy couple, Aquila and his wife Priscilla, who were well-known missionaries in both Corinth and Ephesus. They were a pair, on fire for God. They were partners who allowed Paul to live with them. They traveled with him on a sea journey to Ephesus, where they remained to build up the body of believers. As Paul wrote to the churches in Rome and in Corinth, he always sent greetings and honored this indispensable team. They were instrumental in teaching Apollos, an educator, about the role of the Holy Spirit in the church (Acts 18:24–27). Their home became the "house church" in Ephesus (1 Cor. 16:19).

__Testimony of Truth,__ speak through my life to the power of the Holy Spirit.

ROMANS LIFE LESSONS

ROMANS 1

This is both the longest and the first of Paul's epistles to be written. In it, we find a two-part message of what Christians are to believe and how they are to behave out of their new belief system. He begins with an opening statement of why he put pen to paper in this particular instance. "Paul, a servant of Jesus Christ, called to be an apostle, separated unto the gospel of God, . . . (which he had promised afore by his prophets in the holy scriptures,) Concerning his Son Jesus Christ our Lord, which was made of the seed of David according to the flesh, And declared to be the Son of God with power, according to the Spirit of holiness, by the resurrection from the dead" (Rom. 1:1–4). Paul had never been to Rome. Neither had any of the other disciples. Yet the Word had spread into Rome by those who had been in Jerusalem on the Day of Pentecost. This is the first systematic approach to a Christian's understanding of faith in Christ. It is logical. It is orderly. Its approach is set forth in sequence, listing both blessings and consequences of "right belief." Paul testified to this with boldness. "I am not ashamed of the gospel of Christ: for it is the power of God unto salvation to every one that believeth: to the Jew first, and also to the Greek. For therein is the righteousness of God revealed from faith to faith: as it is written, The just shall live by faith" (Rom. 1:16–17).

> ***Living Testimony,*** *let my life be a witness to the world I touch and affect.*

Paul is adamant in his teaching that "the wrath of God is revealed from heaven against all ungodliness and unrighteousness of men, who hold the truth in unrighteousness, Because that which may be know of God is manifest in them, for God hath shewed it unto them" (Rom. 1:18–19).

The consequences for choosing the wrong god, worshiping the wrong gods, and not turning to the True and Living God has resulted the fact that "wherefore God also gave [humans] up to uncleanness through the lusts of their own hearts, to dishonour their own bodies between themselves: Who changed the truth of God into a lie . . . For this cause God gave them up unto vile affections: for even their women did change the use into that which is against nature . . . God gave them over to a reprobate mind, to do those things . . ." (Rom. 1:24–29). It's a serious indictment! It's a clear statement of how degrading sexual passions came into being. Although Paul is not setting out to specifically deal with particular degrading sexual passions, he provides the underlying reason for perverted sexual relationships: "[they] became vain in their imaginations, and their foolish heart was darkened. Professing themselves to be wise, they became fools, And change the glory of the uncorruptible God into an image made like to corruptible man" (Rom. 1:21–23).

> ***World Wisdom,*** *help me to see You clearly, love You dearly and obey Your will for my life.*

ROMANS 2–3

There is no room for any of us to condemn another. "Thou are inexcusable, O man, whosoever thou are that judgest: for wherein thou judgest another, thou condemnest thyself; for thou that judgest doest the same things" (Rom. 2:1). Although perverted sexual relationships are clearly, for Paul, a result of rebellion against God, Paul does not allow for any of us to "bash and trash" another who continues to live out of their current "wisdom." "For all have sinned, and come short of the glory of God, Being justified freely by his grace through the redemption that is in Christ Jesus: Whom God hath set forth to be a propitiation through faith in his blood" (Rom. 3:23-25).

Atoning Sacrifice, thank You for the blood that bought my pardon.

ROMANS 2-4

"The [promise of God] is of faith, that it might be by grace; to the end the promise might be sure to all the seed; not to that only which is of the law, but that also which is of the faith of Abraham" (Rom. 4:16). There was no Jewish nation when God made a covenant promise with Abram! However, in faith, Abram believed God and a Jewish nation was created through him! Now we, believers, are Jews! "He is not a Jew which is one outwardly; neither is that circumcision, which is outward in the flesh: But he is a Jew, which is one inwardly, and circumcision is that of the heart, in the spirit, and not in the letter" (Rom. 2:28). The Law demanded that all male Jews be circumcised. It showed their distinct difference from other nations. Yet, Jewish women by definition could not perform this rite. Today, however, circumcision of the heart allows us full admittance into the family of God and to the benefits that come with being God's royal heirs!

Great Physician, thank You for the work that You've done within my heart. I know that I've been changed!

ROMANS 16

As Paul drew his letter to a close, he extended personal greetings to folks who had assisted him in various means and those whom he held dear to his heart. It is of great interest that he listed first, Phebe, "a servant of the church" and "a succourer of many." He named a total of nine women: Priscilla, Mary, Junia, Tryphena, Tryphosa, Persis, the mother of Rufus, Julia, and the sister of Nereus. He gave some specifics to a few; Priscilla (and Aquila) fellow workers; Mary, who was a diligent worker; and Tryphena and Tryphosa, hard workers in the Lord. All of these women were intermingled among the names of "brothers" that he greeted as "colaborers" in the ministry of spreading the Word of Jesus Christ. Paul remembered the women, and he did it with fondness and gratitude!

Dear Lord Jesus, use me to spread Your Good News.

1 CORINTHIANS LIFE LESSONS

1 CORINTHIANS 1

The key verse in this letter is found at the beginning of it. "I beseech you, brethren, by the name of our Lord Jesus Christ, that ye speak the same thing, and that there be no divisions among you; but that ye be perfectly joined together in the same mind and in the same judgment" (1:10). Paul proclaims that unity in the church is essential for believers. He does not call for uniformity, for he goes on to declare, "All things are lawful for me, but all things are not expedient: all things are lawful for me, but all things edify not" (10:23). Unity is mandatory for this church in shambles! Ego, pride, immorality, eating meat offered to idols, and internal divisions are just a few of the matters that Paul tries to address in this circulating letter. He attempts once more to teach the believers in Corinth what he had taught them while with them: "For the preaching of the cross is to them that perish foolishness; but unto us which are saved it is the power of God" (1:18). They had argued over who was "the leader" in the church, but Paul refuses to be dragged into that messy situation. "Christ sent me not to baptize, but to preach the gospel: not with wisdom of words, lest the cross of Christ should be made of none effect" (v. 17).

Ultimate Power, may Your resurrection power be displayed in my life.

1 CORINTHIANS 3–5

Paul calls us again to unity by reminding the church, "I have planted, Apollos watered; but God gave the increase" (3:6). We are called to work together for the good of the body. It really makes no difference who gets the credit as long as God gets the glory! "For we are laborers together with God" (v. 9). Paul asks the church: "Know ye not that ye are the temple of God, and that the Spirit of God dwelleth in you?" (v. 16). We are God's dwelling—a sacred holding space for the Holy One to inhabit! How we treat our bodies makes a difference. What we put into our bodies makes a difference. How we act in our bodies makes a difference. The people at Corinth had begun to believe that they were "above" living lives that demonstrated that they were the people of God.

Because of wrong teaching from those who considered themselves wise, they had begun to live lives of great immorality. The result is reported to Paul. "It is reported that there is fornication among you, and such fornication as is not so much as named among the Gentiles, that one should have his father's wife" (5:1). Flagrant sin is rampant and pastor Paul calls it to a quick halt! "Put away from among yourselves that wicked person" (v. 13).

Temple Dwelling God, keep me from immorality. Keep my mind pure.

1 CORINTHIANS 7

In chapter seven as Paul begins to address issues that the Corinthians had brought to his attention, he calls on both men and women in the community to be faithful to marital vows. He is forthright in his call to the sexual rights of each one in the marriage relationship. "Let the husband render unto the wife due benevolence: and likewise also the wife unto the husband" (7:3). In a lengthy discourse on marriage, sex, and divorce, we have a Paul that we hear little of from today's pulpit! In these passages, Paul is an equal-opportunity advocate! Far too many of the Corinthians had gone so far as to abstain from marital sex as a form of rigorous asceticism, which was a "sign" that they had been "delivered" from bodily functions. Paul's pastoral wisdom contradicts this behavior.

> **Spirit of Love,** *keep me holy, in whatever state I find myself.*

1 CORINTHIANS 11–14

Understanding all that Paul wrote about the appropriate behavior of women in the church requires an understanding of the times and the circumstances of the first century. Suffice it to say, that his most often misquoted passage against the role of women in ministry comes from 1 Corinthians 14:32–35, which includes his injunction "Let your women keep silence in the churches . . . they are commanded to be under obedience, as also saith the law" (v. 34). However, it is seldom quoted that prior to this Paul had already said, "Nevertheless neither is the man without the woman, neither the woman without the man, in the Lord. For as the woman is of the man, even so is the man also by the woman; but all things of God" (11:11–12). Paul's whole argument in this letter is based on "the rib" story of Genesis 2.

What happens when you follow the creation story of chapter one of Genesis, where both male and female are created in the image of God? What happens when you recall that Jesus came to women after His resurrection and gave them His message? If women had kept silent at that time, waiting for permission to "speak," would the Good News have been spread to the ends of the earth as Jesus commanded?

Commissioning Christ, thank You for giving us voice and a command to use it in service for your Realm!

2 CORINTHIANS LIFE LESSONS

2 CORINTHIANS 2–5

Paul's advice from the previous letter had not been followed. The problems he had addressed remained. Division in the church continued and now Paul's authority is being questioned further. The letter he had written had been received as a severe rebuke, feelings had been hurt, and anger had flared. Yet Paul remains confident that sinful practices have to cease. "For out of much affliction and anguish of heart I wrote unto you with many tears; not that ye should be grieved, but that ye might know the love which I have more abundantly unto you" (2:4). He asks for forgiveness and forgives the one who had been punished because of his sexual misconduct. He goes to great lengths to discuss the issue of forgiveness "lest Satan should get an advantage of us: for we are not ignorant of his devices" (v. 11). Division is always a problem, even in math! It cannot be left to simply go away. We must work toward reconciliation. Paul leads the way.

We have been given "the ministry of reconciliation" through Christ (5:18). This is a charge we must strive diligently to keep.

> ***Minister of Reconciliation,*** *work this ministry way down on the inside of me. It is so difficult to let go and let God!*

2 CORINTHIANS 6–12

With painful, difficult and often rambling arguments, the apostle Paul struggles to reestablish himself as "an ambassador" and the "official agent" for Jesus Christ who came and brought them the Word of Truth. "Our mouth is open unto you, our heart is enlarged. Ye are not straitened in us, but ye are straitened in your own bowels" (6:11–12). He exhorts them not to heed the counsel of those who challenge his authority and uses chapter 10 to defend himself. "Not to boast in another man's line of things made ready to our hand" (10:16). He charges those causing the divisions with being "false apostles, deceitful workers, transforming themselves into the apostles of Christ" (11:13), and says, "And no marvel; for Satan himself is transformed into an angel of light" (v. 14). He reminds them about Eve, who was "beguiled . . . through [Satan's] subtilty" as the reason for their minds' being led astray from "the simplicity that is in Christ" (v. 3). Yet, Paul goes on to lift up the power of the cross of Christ, which makes redemption possible for all of us. "Most gladly therefore will I rather glory in my infirmities, that the power of Christ may rest upon me. Therefore I take pleasure in infirmities, in reproaches, in necessities, in persecutions, in distresses for Christ's sake: for when I am weak, then am I strong" (12:9–10). We thrive because of the cross. Paul also admonishes us to "be of good comfort, be of one mind, live in peace; and the God of love and peace shall with you" (13:11). Isn't that good news?

> *May "the grace of the Lord Jesus Christ, and the love of God, and the communion of the Holy Ghost" be with us all! (13:14)*

GALATIANS LIFE LESSONS

GALATIANS 1–3

Paul understood being misunderstood and attacked. His teachings were undermined by those known as Judaizers. These Judaizers taught the Galatians that in order for them to be "true" Christians, they had to follow all the constraints of the Law of Moses. Chapters one and two reaffirm Paul's authority as "an apostle, (not of men, neither by man, but by Jesus Christ, and God the Father, who raised him from the dead)" (1:1) and detail his systematic theology of freedom in Christ. In chapter three, he asks the essential question, "O foolish Galatians, who hath bewitched you, that ye should not obey the truth...?" (v. 1).

The "new" teachers persuaded the Christians that circumcision and other rites were necessary to achieve salvation. However, Paul reminds them, "He therefore that ministereth to you the Spirit, and worketh miracles among you, doeth he it by the works of the law, or by the hearing of faith?" (3:5). He also asserts, "But after that faith is come, we are no longer under a schoolmaster" (v. 25). In other words, we are no longer under the supervision of the Law. Paul then writes: "Ye are all the children of God by faith in Christ Jesus. For as many of you as have been baptized into Christ have put on Christ. There is neither Jew nor Greek, there is neither bond nor free, there is neither male nor female: for ye are all one in Christ Jesus" (vv. 26–28).

Adopting and Accepting God, I give You thanks for making me an heir to the promise made to Abraham and Sarah. Through Jesus Christ, I am included!

GALATIANS 4

As he tries to reach the hearts and spirits of this confused congregation, Paul uses the metaphor of his being "the mother" of this people. "My little children, of whom I travail in birth again until Christ be formed in you, I desire to be present with you now, and to change my voice; for I stand in doubt of you" (4:19–20).

Loving God, help me in my times of confusion to feel Your mother-like concern for me.

EPHESIANS LIFE LESSONS

EPHESIANS 1–5

Chapter one begins this letter of encouragement as Paul greets the saints and offers thanksgiving and prayer for their faithful response to the good news of Jesus Christ. He reminds them that "we all had our conversation in times past in the lusts of our flesh, fulfilling the desires of the flesh and of the mind; and were by nature the children of wrath, even as others. But God, who is rich in mercy, for his great love wherewith he loved us, even when we were dead in sins, hath quickened us together with Christ, (by grace ye are saved;)" (2:3–5). Paul then details the unity of Jews and Gentiles in the body of Christ: "For he is our peace, who hath made both one, and hath broken down the middle wall of partition between us; having abolished in his flesh the enmity, even the law of commandments contained in ordinances; for to make in himself of twain one new man, so making peace" (vv. 14–15). His prayer is that the Ephesians will "walk worthy of the vocation wherewith ye are called" (4:1). He appeals to them as a "prisoner of the Lord" (v. 1) and calls for them to live lives of righteousness to "grieve not the holy Spirit of God" (v. 30). Paul then admonishes, "Be ye therefore followers of God, as dear children" (5:1). They are to "[submit] yourselves one to another in the fear of God" (v. 21). That's good advice!

> *Lord of All, to Thee we raise our humble voice of grateful praise for Your amazing love.*

PHILIPPIANS LIFE LESSONS

PHILIPPIANS 1

Chapter one introduces us to "Paul and Timotheus, the servants of Jesus Christ" (1:1). Paul gives God thanks for the people in Philippi who have entered into partnership with them on behalf of the Good News (v. 3–4, 7). Paul mentions his confidence that the Lord would continue to work in the hearts of the Philippian believers (v. 6). The Philippians worked in different ways to assure that the ministry was advanced. They had not only witnessed in Philippi but also helped to support the traveling team of Paul and Timothy. Paul wants them to understand that his imprisonment has not hindered the work of God. Instead: "many of the brethren in the Lord, waxing confident by my bonds, are much more bold to speak the word without fear" (v. 14). Here Paul helps us to understand that our circumstances can always promote the Good News. Our attitude, which shapes how we handle situations which life brings our way, can give glory and honor to God.

> *Joy Giver, let me always rejoice in Your ability to bring me through difficult situations. Keep me focused on You.*

PHILIPPIANS 4

We are provided with a vivid portrait of women at work in the church at Philippi. In chapter four, Paul pleads with Euodias and Syntyche "be of the same mind in the Lord" (v. 2).

"My brethren dearly beloved and longed for . . . I intreat thee also, true yokefellow, help those women which laboured with me in the gospel, with Clement also, and with other my fellowlabourers, whose names are in the book of life" (4:1, 3). This admonition from Paul gives us a different view of his appreciation, respect, and acceptance of women involved in the ministry of the local church. There is no doubt we have the names of "sisters" because he specifically requests, "help those women." What is essential for us to note is that the women, whose influence has helped the growth of the church, have a broken relationship that has been brought to the attention of Paul.

These are not unnamed women, but we know that Euodias and Syntyche have had a significant falling out which has not been reconciled. As Paul writes about joy in Christ, he begs for reconciliation between the sisters. It is imperative, if we desire abiding joy in our life that we not get caught up in the "E & S" syndrome of petty infighting, which detracts from our witness.

> ***Great One,*** *let us always remember our unity in the body. Keep us mindful that You have more than enough love to go around for every sibling!*

Paul concludes his letter by giving thanks to the congregation for the great contribution they have sent through Epaphroditus. Telling them "whatsoever things are true, whatsoever things are honest, whatsoever things are just, whatsoever things are pure, whatsoever things are lovely, whatsoever things are of good report; if there be any virtue, and if there be any praise, think on these things" (4:8). He thanks them and shares with them that he "[has] learned, in whatever state [he is], therewith to be content" (v. 11), all because "I can do all things through Christ which strengtheneth me" (v. 13). He concludes by greeting them in the name of Christ Jesus and sending them hellos; "all the saints salute you, chiefly they that are of Caesar's household" (v. 22). This reminds them that even in jail, he is winning souls for Christ! There is no spot that Christ is not!

> *Lord, may we always be aware of the privilege of being able to say to another, "the grace of the Lord Jesus Christ be with you all. Amen" (v. 23).*

COLOSSIANS LIFE LESSONS

COLOSSIANS 1–2

Colossians, Philippians, Ephesians, and Philemon are called the Prison Letters, written while Paul was jailed in Rome.

The greeting to this letter is an identification and authority of the apostle (1:1–2). This is followed by a prayer of thanksgiving for their love, faith, and hope—the cornerstones of Christianity (vv. 3–8). Knowledge is not listed until he prays for them to be filled with the knowledge of God's perfect will through belief in Jesus Christ (vv. 9–10). For Paul, it was a time to reinforce the fact that "what" one knew was not as important as "who" one knew. The One to know was Jesus Christ.

Knowledge had become a central focus of controversy in the church. Paul lifts up the supremacy of Christ, who "is the image of the invisible God, the firstborn over all creation. For by him were all things created, that are in heaven, and that are in earth . . . He is before all things, and by him all things consist. And he is the head of the body, the church" (vv. 15–18). Paul is well aware of the "enticing words" (2:4) being taught which declared that secret knowledge was being withheld from most believers. The Gnostics also taught that body was evil and that Jesus had only appeared to be human but was not. Paul encourages the saints to "beware lest any man spoil you through philosophy and vain deceit, after the tradition of men, after the rudiments of the world, and not after Christ" (v. 8).

> ***Christ of All,*** *keep me firmly rooted in my belief that You alone are sufficient for my salvation. Let the world and its traditions not invade and cloud my mind.*

COLOSSIANS 3

Paul exhorts the saints: "If ye then be risen with Christ, seek those things which are above, where Christ sitteth on the right hand of God. Set your affection on things above, not on things on the earth" (3:1–2). He goes on to describe rules for right living for believers to follow. He instructs us to take off the old sinful garments and to put on the new clothing, which comes from a relationship with Jesus Christ (vv. 12–14). He gives us a basic Christian Education program to work through. He talks about the need for forgiveness to be at work in us so that reconciliation and unity might be evident for all to see. "Above all these things put on charity, which is the bond of perfectness. And let the peace of God rule in your hearts" (vv. 14–15). Forgiveness is the key! When we remember that God loved us enough to forgive us for our sinful nature and practices, it ought to make it easier to forgive others for their sins against us. Forgiveness requires diligence and practice.

> ***Forgiving God,*** *help me to always remember Your willingness to forgive me!*

COLOSSIANS 4

Paul concludes his letter with firm instructions: "Continue in prayer, and watch in the same with thanksgiving; withal praying also for us" (4:2–3). He uplifts the brothers and sisters ministering in Laodicea, especially noting "Nymphas, and the church which is in his house" (v. 15). Finally, he sends a firm warning to Archippus and to each of us! "Say to Archippus, Take heed to the ministry which thou hast received in the Lord, that thou fulfil it" (v. 17). Too many of us know what God has called us to do, but allow other people and situations to retard our progress with a given assignment. It is clear that Archippus had started doing something that had the potential to be significant within the life of the church. However, he had stopped working. We are each given specific roles to play within the body. This is the function of spiritual gifts (see 2 Cor. 12). When we don't do our job, others suffer! See to it that you complete the work you have received in the Lord!

Assigning Savior, You finished Your job on a rugged tree on Calvary. Despite the suffering and agony, You did not stop. Help me to get up and get busy. Help me to finish my task with joy!

1 THESSALONIANS LIFE LESSONS

1 THESSALONIANS 2

Paul writes to people who had suffered persecution for their faith. As he recalls his time with the believers at Thessalonica, after offering thanksgiving for their steadfast faith, he reminds them, "We might have been burdensome, as the apostles of Christ. But we were gentle among you, even as a nurse cherisheth her children: So being affectionately desirous of you, we were willing to have imparted unto you, not the gospel of God only, but also our own souls, because ye were dear unto us" (2:6–8). Here Paul does not resort to "manly power" to lord over the church. He affirms the womanly qualities of gentleness and the ability to share, like a loving mother. Relationships among the people of Christ must always be characterized by a gentle spirit that exhibits love.

> ***Gentle Redeemer,*** *work the quality of gentleness throughout my relationships, especially the very difficult ones!*

1 THESSALONIANS 4

Paul tells the believers that "This is the will of God, even your sanctification, that ye should abstain from fornication: That every one of you should know how to possess his vessel in sanctification and honour; Not in the lust of concupiscence, even as the Gentiles which know not God. . . . For God hath not called us unto uncleanness, but unto holiness" (4:3–5, 7). Keeping our bodies under subjection is not always easy. Yet it is required. It is possible with the help of the Holy Spirit. A holy life honors God. Unfortunately, sexual sin was an expected and accepted way of life in the Greco-Roman world.

God calls us to live at a higher standard. To be sanctified

means to be set apart for Christ through the Holy Spirit working in us to bring us into conformity with the will of God—not in conformity with the low standards of the world.

> *Sanctifying Spirit, move me to do God's perfect will.*

1 THESSALONIANS 5

When the going gets rough there must be a place and a community where comfort and solace may be found. Paul knew firsthand the severity of the suffering being experienced by the church. Therefore, he encouraged them to "comfort yourselves together, and edify one another, even as also ye do" (5:11). The gift of encouragement is a necessary one for the church of God today. If it's missing in your local assembly, perhaps it can start with you!

> *Lord, this is my prayer for all I know: May "the very God of peace sanctify you wholly; and I pray God your whole spirit and soul and body be preserved blameless unto the coming of our Lord Jesus Christ. Faithful is he that calleth you, who also will do it" (vv. 23–24).*

2 THESSALONIANS LIFE LESSONS

2 THESSALONIANS 2-3

Much of what we heard and read in Paul's first letter is repeated as he attempts to clarify his teachings. "Remember ye not, that, when I was yet with you, I told you these things?" (2:5) "Therefore, brethren, stand fast, and hold the traditions which ye have been taught, whether by word, or our epistle. Now our Lord Jesus Christ himself, and God, even our Father, which hath loved us, and hath given us everlasting consolation and good hope through grace, comfort your hearts, and stablish you in every good word and work" (vv. 15-17). Paul realizes that some of the congregation has grown weary of the unceasing persecution of the church. The words of encouragement are repeated in order to strengthen believers for the difficult days ahead. Apathy is to be expected when difficulties continue. It is a defense mechanism, which allows us to let down our guards and be further deceived by the enemy of our souls! "But the Lord is faithful, who shall stablish you, and keep you from evil" (3:3) Our faithfulness is the expected response.

> *Faithful One,* hard times cause me to seek ways of escape. Help me to remain faithful to You.

Those who anticipated the immediate return of Christ used this as an excuse to cease working. They became a burden to the rest of the community. Paul calls the church to remember that "when we were with you, this we commanded you, that if any would not work, neither should he eat" (3:10). The church should not support the lazy. This speaks to women who allow adult sons to return home without making every attempt to find gainful employment. It surely addresses those sisters who allow adult men—significant others—to live in their homes without working. If we do this, we're supporting and encouraging that man's sinful habits.

> **The grace of our Lord Jesus Christ** be with [us] all! (v. 18)

1 TIMOTHY LIFE LESSONS

1 TIMOTHY 1

As Paul writes to a younger man who pastors the church Paul had founded in Ephesus, he reflects upon the grace of God: "And I thank Christ Jesus our Lord, who hath enabled me, for that he counted me faithful, putting me into the ministry; Who was before a blasphemer, and a persecutor, and injurious: but I obtained mercy, because I did it ignorantly in unbelief. And the grace of our Lord was exceeding abundant with faith and love which is in Christ Jesus. This is a faithful saying, and worthy of all acceptation, that Christ Jesus came into the world to save sinners; of whom I am chief. Howbeit for this cause I obtained mercy, that in me first Jesus Christ might shew forth all longsuffering, for a pattern to them which should hereafter believe on him to life everlasting" (1:12–16). Paul chooses not to begin his teaching from an exalted position of seniority, but by recalling where grace found him as he persecuted the people of God! (See Acts 7:58; 9:1–2.)

__Amazing Grace,__ thank You for loving, choosing and using a sinner like me!

1 TIMOTHY 2

Chapter two provides instructions on the order of worship. "I exhort therefore, that, first of all, supplications, prayers, intercessions, and giving of thanks, be made for all men; For kings, and for all that are in authority; that we may lead a quiet and peaceable life in all godliness" (2:1–2). In a time period when severe persecutions are taking place, praying for "peace and quiet" is wise.

Paul also provides instructions about the dress of women. The following verses about women in the church are included: "Let the woman learn in silence with all subjection. But I suffer not a woman to teach, nor to usurp authority over the man, but to be in silence" (vv. 11–12). This passage must be interpreted in light of Paul's statement that there is "neither male nor female" in the Body of Christ. (See Galatians 3:28.)

> ***Supreme Guide,*** *help me worship You in spirit and in truth!*

1 TIMOTHY 5

In chapter five, Paul's advice encompasses widows, elder, and servants. Paul admonishes Timothy to "honour widows that are widows indeed. But if any widow have children or nephews, let them learn first to shew piety at home, and to requite their parents: for that is good and acceptable before God" (5:2–3). In other words, Paul suggests that families help support the widows. As we would say today, "Charity begins at home!" Real piety or devotion for God can be seen in one's actions. After all, "faith without works is dead" (James 2:26). This is not to say that one has to earn salvation by works. Rather, one shows her obedience to God by her actions.

> ***Provider of the widowed,*** *let me not overlook those in need, whether they are in my family or in my community.*

2 TIMOTHY LIFE LESSONS

2 TIMOTHY 1

Facing death for his life as a follower of Jesus, the apostle Paul writes, "passing the torch" to "Timothy, my dearly beloved son" (1:2). Persecution under Nero is in full swing; Paul is imprisoned and awaiting execution. He writes to Timothy to encourage him to keep the faith and carry out the ministry at his hand without apology. Reminding Timothy of "the unfeigned faith that is in thee, which dwelt first in thy grandmother Lois, and thy mother," Paul urges this younger man to "stir up the gift of God, which is in thee by the putting on of my hands. For God hath not given us the spirit of fear; but of power, and of love, and of a sound" (vv. 5–7).

> ***Spirit of Power,*** *Love and Sound Mind, live strong in me!*

2 TIMOTHY 2

Giving a young man the wisdom of both his years and live experience, Paul attempts to provide Timothy with a manual for church administration. Paul knew Timothy would need grace in abundance. So, he writes, "Be strong in the grace that is in Christ Jesus" (2:1). This is a reminder to Timothy to trust completely in the undeserved favor and merit of the One who was "of the seed of David was raised from the dead" (v. 8). As an elder in the church Paul charges Timothy to "put them in remembrance . . . Study to shew thyself approved unto God, a workman that needeth not to be ashamed, rightly dividing the word of truth" (vv. 14–15). Vital leaders are those who remain faithful and diligent to the reading, studying, internalizing, and living of the Word of God.

> ***Living Word,*** *speak to my heart. Give me the words that will bring new life.*

2 TIMOTHY 3

There will be difficult days ahead, Paul assures Timothy. "For men shall be lovers of their own selves, covetous, boasters, proud, blasphemers, disobedient to parents, unthankful, unholy, . . . lovers of pleasures more than lovers of God; having a form of godliness, but denying the power thereof: from such turn away" (3:2–5). This passage warns Timothy about the false teachers who come with untruth and cause women to abandon the faith (v. 6). Since women were not allowed formal education, their study was limited to what was taught in the house churches. Many false teachers led women astray. To be called "silly" (v. 6) might sound insulting; nevertheless, it's true today! We need to be grounded in God's truth in Jesus Christ in order that we might not be fooled by good-looking, nice-sounding liars who claim to speak for God!

> *Spirit of Truth,* teach me wisdom so that I might discern truth from error.

2 TIMOTHY 4

Paul closes his letter with a final greeting. "Salute Prisca and Aquila" (4:19). Prisca "is mentioned first, which perhaps indicates her greater importance among Christians, since normally in antiquity the person with greater status—the man, for example, or the person with a higher social class—would be named first" (WBC, 359–60). At the end of his life, Paul remembers those who have worked faithfully with him, prayerfully supported him, and sustained him with lodging and financial assistance. He had given his life for the sake of the Gospel and he recognized that many others had interwoven their lives with his. Community was important to the apostle Paul. It was another piece of the legacy he left for his son in Christ, Timothy.

> *Weaving God,* let the threads of my life be knit with others who are working to cover the world with a tapestry of love in the blessed name of Your Son, Jesus Christ.

TITUS
LIFE LESSONS

TITUS 1–2

Leadership in the church is Paul's agenda. Titus is a Gentile, a Greek who of great assistance to Paul between his first and second imprisonments in Rome. After a typical "Pauline" greeting, acknowledging Titus as "mine own son after the common faith" (v. 4), we are not left in doubt about the purpose of this letter. "For this cause I left thee in Crete, that thou shouldest set in order the things that are wanting, and ordain elders in every city, as I had appointed thee" (v. 5). Because "one of themselves, even a prophet of their own, said, The Cretans are always liars, evil beasts, slow bellies. This witness is true. Wherefore rebuke them sharply, that they may be sound in the faith" (v. 12). This "storm" of wrong doctrine had to be dealt with. The Judaizers taught the new Gentile converts that they had to be followers of Jewish Law before they could be Christians. Paul wants these converts to receive the truth. "But speak thou the things which become sound" (2:1).

> *Source of Truth,* lead me in the way everlasting. Let my leadership be a model worthy of emulation, I pray.

TITUS 2

Duties for various members in the church are outlined. The older men and women are listed. Young men are instructed. Younger women are called to "love their husbands, to love their children, to be discreet, chaste, keepers at home, good, obedient to their own husbands, that the word of God be not blasphemed" (2:4–5). Titus is challenged to teach the young men in order "that he that is of the contrary part may be ashamed, having no evil thing to say of you" (v. 8). Titus also is to "exhort servants to be obedient unto their own masters, and to please them well in all things . . . that they may adorn the doctrine of God our Savior in all" (vv. 9–10).

***Liberating Savior,** thank You for the power to live a life that is pleasing to You.*

PHILEMON LIFE LESSONS

PHILEMON 1

Paul begins this short letter by greeting a friend and co-laborer, Apphia, whom scholars believe was a female patron of the house church. She is called "beloved" (v. 2). This is not a meaningless designation from Paul. This title indicates that Apphia has been greatly involved and even highly influential in the spread of the Gospel in Colossse. Apphia also may have been Philemon's wife.

> Paul's strategy is to use persons (Beloved Apphia and our fellow soldier, Archippus, v. 2) who are Philemon's equals as well as the larger community as an audience who will judge whether or not Philemon has taken the apostle's advice. (WBC, 362)

Paul is wise enough and skilled enough to pull out all the stops when it comes to having Onesimus treated as a member of the Body of Christ. The matter was serious enough for Brother Paul to ask Sister Apphia for help!

> ***Connecting Bond of Love,*** *thank You for allowing the sisterhood to be of assistance in the spread of Your Good News for the entire family.*

Paul called Philemon "brother" (v. 20) after calling him a beloved friend and fellow laborer (v. 2). He addresses Onesimus, a slave, as his "son" (v. 10) and "beloved brother" (v. 20). He does not speak against slavery, which is an accepted practice of the culture, but instead admonishes Philemon to "receive him for ever; not now as a servant, but above a servant, a brother beloved (vv. 15–16). The connection Paul uses is that of family. It is not simply a family of origin, one in which we have no choice, but it is the family of blood ties! For the shed blood of Jesus connected us at the cross. Paul renames the relationships and redefines the boundaries. "If thou count me therefore a partner, receive him as myself" (v. 17). Onesimus is uplifted by Paul as his equal. Philemon is called upon to do the same.

> ***God of All,*** *to Thee we raise this our voice of grateful praise for being part of Your beloved family.*

HEBREWS LIFE LESSONS

HEBREWS 1–2

In chapter one, the writer of Hebrews explains that the New Covenant was come, thanks to the coming of Christ. In chapter two, the author urges that the people of the Way avoid returning to their old beliefs and habits of depending upon rituals as a way to establish a relationship with God. He reminds them that Jesus is superior to the angels (1:4; 2:5–18). Jesus is "gooder than good." The best of the "old" covenant could not compare to Jesus. "But we see Jesus, who was made a little lower than the angels for the suffering of death, crowned with glory and honour; that he by the grace of God should taste death for every man" (2:9).

> ***Taster of Death,*** *thank You for taking the victory from the jaws of death for me!*

HEBREWS 4

"Let us therefore come boldly unto the throne of grace, that we may obtain mercy, and find grace to help in time of need" (4:16). This is one of those verses we need to commit to memory for the hard times. There is no spot where God is not, and there is nothing too hard for Him! This verse assures us that that we can't wear out God's grace or mercy. Every time we approach God's throne, His grace and mercy is also there to cover our sins. And, when we come seeking intervention, we don't have to come begging. We are to come with bold confidence that our God is more than able to assist us.

> ***Jehovah-jireh,*** *my Provider, You have more than enough to meet my every need!*

HEBREWS 5

"We have many things to say, and hard to be uttered, seeing ye are dull of hearing" (5:11). Sometimes a rebuke is necessary to get one's point across. Instead of being able to write more about Jesus' role as High Priest, the author is forced to cease because the readers are "dull of hearing." In other words, they were slow to learn or slow to make progress in their Christian walk. May this never be said of us!

> ***Patient Instructor,*** *help me not to be satisfied with where I am in my walk with You. Instead, may I have joy in growing more and more like You.*

HEBREWS 10

The superiority of Christ and the superiority of faith in Christ are repeated over and over again as an encouragement against returning to the old familiar rituals and patterns of worship. "Sacrifice and offering thou wouldest not . . . in burnt offerings and sacrifices for sin thou hast had no pleasure" (10:5–6). "Cast not away therefore your confidence, which hath great recompence of reward" (v. 35). The saints are encouraged to hold on to their faith despite the persecution that continues. "But we are not of them who draw back unto perdition; but of them that believe to the saving of the soul" (v. 39).

Promise Keeper, I holding onto my faith in every promise You have made.

HEBREWS 11

The chapter is known as the "Hebrews Hall of Faith." The words "by faith" in many of the verses in this chapter call to mind an image of an active faith. This famous chapter is both a litany and roll call for the patriarchs and matriarchs of our Christian faith. It includes flesh-and-blood men and women who were risk takers for God. None of them had faith in what they could literally see. They made it to these pages of ancient history due to their faith in the precious promises of God. "These all died in the faith, not having received the promises, but having see them afar off, and were persuaded of them, and embraced them, and confessed that they were strangers and pilgrims on the earth" (11:13). We find the names of precious few women. Among those mentioned are Sara (v. 11); Jochebed, the mother of Moses (v. 23; she is not named here, however); the nameless Pharaoh's daughter who named Moses (v. 24); and Rahab, the harlot (v. 31). A fascinating sentence is found in verse 35: "Women received their dead raised to life again." This includes many sisters in Old Testament Scriptures as well as those who encountered both Jesus and the apostles (see, for example, Luke 7:11–17). Their names are not called, but their faith is noted for us today! They did it because "God having provided some better thing for us, that they without us should not be made perfect" (v. 40).

Faithful One, help me to be a woman who actually lives by my words of faith.

HEBREWS 13

"Let brotherly love continue. Be not forgetful to entertain strangers: for thereby some have entertained angels unawares" (13:1–2). Love includes the stranger, regards the nameless, and is hospitable to everyone without regard for status. Hospitality is a spiritual gift! Hospitality is a mark of the average woman of color. This ability to include others within the open circle of our love is a good example of the way God has drawn the circle wider to pull us inside.

Grace Greater Than All Our Sin, thank You for including us!

JAMES LIFE LESSONS

JAMES 1

James is the "wisdom" epistle of the New Testament. It is filled with practical advice for living as a Christian ought. For James, a "living faith" is essential to make a difference in the world. Since he is fully aware of the persecutions against the people of the Way (Christians), he does not begin this letter with false hope and chitchat. Also, he does not offer the slightest possibility that the living for Christ will ever get any easier! He assumes that trials, persecution, and death are part of the lifestyle of Jesus' people. "Count it all joy when ye fall into divers temptations; knowing this, that the trying of your faith worketh patience. But let patience have her perfect work, that ye may be perfect and entire, wanting nothing. If any of you lack wisdom, let him ask of God, that giveth to all men liberally, and upbraideth not" (1:2–5). It's not a matter of "if" we will face severe challenges, but "when" we do. James exhorts us to go to God for help to make it through each trial. Wisdom will be our guide through the storms of life that are sure to come and will continue to come.

> ***Wisdom of the Ages,*** *fill me with directions and instructions to steer me through the storms of my life.*

JAMES 2

Chapter two says that genuine faith forbids favoritism. This chapter is not couched in theological language. James says simply, "My brethren, have not the faith of our Lord Jesus Christ, the Lord of glory, with respect of persons" (2:1).

> *James addressed Christians who were experiencing community conflict that had reached crisis proportions. The root cause of this crisis seems to have been the community's adoption of questionable social values derived from the world rather than from God's law. (Cain Hope Felder,* Troubling Biblical Waters *[Maryknoll, NY: Orbis Press, 1997], 118–120)*

Lifter of Our Heads, *thank You for not showing favoritism but counting me as Your own.*

"Shew me thy faith without thy works, and I will shew thee my faith by my works ... Abraham believed God, and it was imputed unto him for righteousness: and he was called the Friend of God. ... Likewise also was not Rahab the harlot justified by works, when she had received the messengers, and had sent them out another way?" (2:18, 23–25). James calls for us to "put up or shut up"! Empty words, reciting creeds of faith, carelessly mouthing Scriptures, and speaking Christian vernacular do not a Christian make! Rahab, the prostitute who shielded the spies as the Israelites entered the Promised Land (Josh. 2) is used as an example of how a "living faith" works (v. 25).

Savior of Sinners, help my walk to match my talk in every circumstance.

JAMES 4

Submission is a Christian virtue. Our true submission is unto God. "God resisteth the proud, but giveth grace unto the humble. Submit yourselves therefore to God. Resist the devil, and he will flee from you. Draw nigh to God, and he will draw nigh to you. Cleanse your hands, ye sinners; and purify your hearts, ye double minded.... Humble yourselves in the sight of the Lord, and he shall lift you up" (4:6–10). Submission—yielding and committing our whole selves, mind, body, and soul—brings us near to the heart of God. Many of us, especially women of color, have great difficulty with the phrase "humble yourselves" in verse 10. What we need to remember is that the word humble in the Greek language of the New Testament does not mean "doormat"! To be humble is to recognize that our worth comes from God alone. It means that we know that we are solely dependent on God. We live, move, and have our being in God. Knowing this helps us understand that we are not independent nor are we left alone. We are wholly dependent upon the grace of a loving, long-suffering and beneficent God. It's all right to be humble under the mighty hand of the Almighty!

Merciful and Beneficent One, I bow in humble submission with awe and reverence.

JAMES 5

"Is any among you afflicted? let him pray. Is any merry? let him sing psalms. Is any sick among you? let him call for the elders of the church; and let them pray over him, anointing him with oil in the name of the Lord: And the prayer of faith shall save the sick, and the Lord shall raise him up; and if he hath committed sins, they shall be forgiven him. Confess your faults one to another, and pray one for another, that ye may be healed. The effectual fervent prayer of a righteous man availeth much" (5:13–16). Prayer is our most powerful resource. Too many times we do all that we can do first and resort to prayer as a "last resort"! James gives us a formula for which results are guaranteed. A key portion of being "raised up" (v. 15) is confession, which means to agree with God's Word about where you are at the moment. "Confess your faults one to another" (v. 16). This is not a call to empty out all the various sinful things you have done to everyone. But it is a call to find those who are trusted and proven intercessors who can receive your confession without judgment, but in grace pray with you for a place of restoration. All of us reach a place of brokenness in the realm of our spiritual lives. During these times, the presence of God might seem absent. This is a time to call for the saints and to share your brokenness. For the promise is that "the Lord shall raise him up." It is your privilege. It is God's will for us to be whole. Follow the formula and benefit from God's divine intervention in your situations.

Healing God, pour Your oil of anointing upon my head. Let it run down like the needed rain. Let it overflow the dry places in my life. Anointing, fall on me!

1 PETER LIFE LESSONS

1 PETER 1

This letter is addressed to "the strangers scattered throughout Pontus, Galatia, Cappadocia, Asia, and Bithynia, elect according to the foreknowledge of God the Father" (1:1–2). Our ancestors used to sing a spiritual that goes, "I'm just a stranger here, heaven is my home." They were assured of the fact that suffering came for only a season and that they had "an inheritance incorruptible, and undefiled, and that fadeth not away, reserved in heaven for you, who are kept by the power of God through faith unto salvation ready to be revealed in the last time" (1:4–5). Through the tribulations and persecution of slavery, our ancestors realized that God prepared them for something better in the homeland of their soul. That's why they could sing with gusto and conviction, "One glad morning, when this life is over, I will fly away and be at rest!" "Wherefore gird up the loins of your mind, be sober, and hope to the end for the grace that is to be brought unto you at the revelation of Jesus Christ; As obedient children, not fashioning yourselves according to the former lusts in your ignorance.... Be holy in all manner of" (vv. 13–15). It's easy to retaliate and do "tit for tat" living when you know the oppressor! Yet Peter calls for a higher standard. For you have been "born again!" (v. 23).

__Strong Deliverer,__ You are worthy to be praised for preparing us for new life in Your Kingdom.

1 PETER 2

"Ye are a chosen generation, a royal priesthood, an holy nation, a peculiar people; that ye should shew forth the praises of him who hath called you out of darkness into his marvelous light: which in time past were not a people, but are now the people of God" (2:9–10). What a high privilege to be adopted into a royal family. Adoption comes not as a result of our doing. Our noteworthy accomplishments, class backgrounds, our gender or our ethnic group will never bring us to this status before God! God chose us. Christ redeemed us. And the Holy Spirit is at work in us, with us and on our behalf to win others as "they may by your good works, which they shall behold, glorify God" (v. 12).

__King of Glory,__ be glorified in my life.

1 PETER 3

God does not need, want or desire "CIA Christians." CIA Christians are undercover Christians. God does not want cowards as witnesses to His glory. God allows our trials to come and uses them to evidence our trust in Him. That's why in the midst of a trial or after we have gained victory, Peter reminds us to "be ready always to give an answer to every man that asketh you a reason of the hope that is in you with meekness and fear" (3:15). Storms are coming. The world is watching how we go through our storms. Let them see through our lifestyle that our hope is anchored in the One who turned a cross into a symbol of victorious triumph!

> *Seer of All Things,* may I be willing *"to give an answer to every man that asketh" concerning the hope that is in me (v. 15).*

1 PETER 4

"The end of all things is a t hand: be ye therefore sober, and watch unto prayer. And above al things have fervent charity among yourselves: for charity shall cover the multitude of sins" (4:7–8). This love is not an erotic, self-absorbed feeling. This love is not even a "family" type, a certain attitude of "I've got to love them, but I sure don't like them." This love is God's accepting, selfless love that goes beyond "I've done all I'm willing to do" to "what more can I do?" We are impoverished in the English language and use the word love very loosely. We "love" clothes, hairdos, and nail colors! Peter calls us to use the love of God when dealing with each other. This will end the petty infighting that crops up so easily between sisters. God is love. And God has enough love for each of us in the family. Let love hide the faults of the individual you are most angry with today. Ask God to allow love to hide your faults as you "work" somebody else's nerve!

> *Lover of My Soul,* let me to Your bosom fly as I seek the love which hides others' faults!

2 PETER LIFE LESSONS

2 PETER 1

This letter is a warning against false teachers who try to undermine the teachings of Jesus Christ. "His divine power hath given unto us all things that pertain unto life and godliness, through the knowledge of him that hath called us to glory and virtue: Whereby are given unto us exceeding great and precious promises . . . For we have not followed cunningly devised fables, when we made known unto you the power and coming of our Lord Jesus Christ, but were eyewitnesses of his majesty" (1:3–4, 16). We are not telling lies, spinning yarns, or engaging in fairy tales, says Peter.

Lying teachers instructed that self-control in sexual matters was not necessary since the body and its deeds were not important. Peter admonishes, "Add to your faith virtue; and to virtue knowledge; and to knowledge temperance; and to temperance patience... for if these things be in you, and abound, they make you that ye shall neither be barren not unfruitful in the knowledge of our Lord Jesus Christ" (vv. 5–6, 8). A living, dynamic faith is one controlled by the work of the Holy Spirit in us, bringing glory to God in all we do. It is essential that we "give diligence to make your calling and election sure: for if ye do these things, ye shall never fall: for so an entrance shall be ministered unto you abundantly into the everlasting kingdom of our Lord and Savior Jesus Christ" (v. 10). Sisters, self-control is not an option!

***Spirit of Truth,** lead me in ways that are life giving and glory producing!*

2 PETER 1–3

Peter spends the first chapter of this epistle giving us a "math lesson"—qualities to add to our faith (1:5–7). These qualities will keep a believer discerning—a necessary commodity when false teachers are about! Peter's argument that "if God spared not the angels that sinned, but cast them down to hell, and delivered them into chains of darkness, to be reserved unto judgment" (2:4) demonstrates that God is going to punish those who deceive Christians and lead them into sin and error. "Through covetousness shall they with feigned words make merchandise of you" (v. 3). We need to evaluate our teachers and what they are teaching. All teachings should measure up to the Word of God. It makes no difference how good these teachings sounds. We are called to be careful about what teachings we allow to guide our conduct, especially our sexual conduct. If it sounds too good to be true, most likely it's not! "Therefore, beloved, seeing ye know these things before, beware . . . grow in the grace, and in the knowledge of our Lord and Savior Jesus Christ" (3:17–18).

Wise Counselor, guide me to know Your truth.

I JOHN LIFE LESSONS

1 JOHN 1

John writes to remind us that Jesus is the Light. He talks of his own personal witness to the Living Christ. "We have seen with our eyes, which we have looked upon, and out hands have handled, of the Word of life . . . We have seen it, and bear witness, and shew unto you that eternal life" (1:1–2). Declining commitment to the practices taught by Jesus prompts John's letter. John writes to correct error in judgment and behaviors among those calling themselves

Christians yet living by lower standards. His letter includes words of loving encouragement for true believers. He begins with two strong references to his lasting impressions of Jesus, that of "Light" and "Living Word." John testifies to what he has seen and experienced. This is what we are called to do!

***Light of the World,** shine in me and through me that others will know that my experience with You is authentic and enduring.*

1 JOHN 2

"Love not the world, neither the things that are in the world. . . . For all that is in the world, the lust of the flesh, and the lust of the eyes, and the pride of life, is not of the Father, but is of the world" (2:15–16). John writes to assist us in severing our strong and fatal attachment to the "strings" of the world. He deals with inward cravings—the pull toward things that are not satisfying or eternal. He refers us back to the Garden of Eden where Adam and Eve craved equality with God, looked at the forbidden tree, and yielded to temptation and sin. The tricks of the enemy of our soul has not changed! The things or objects may be different, but John warns us to be on the alert.

***Eternal Life,** keep me focused on You!*

1 JOHN 3

"For this is the message that ye heard from the beginning, that we should love one another" (3:11). The message of Jesus is constant (see John 13:34). It is a message of loving embrace and inclusion. Love is not a warm, fuzzy feeling that comes when others behave in ways we find acceptable. Love is not an ego-satisfying impulse that seeks to dominate another. The love of Jesus is a sharing, empowering, accepting activity which as constant and consistent, born of His self-giving nature. Jesus is love in action. His actions were and are those of generosity, healing, and inclusion. We are called to a consistency in our thoughts and behaviors.

Love Incarnate, live through me.

1 JOHN 4

"Beloved, believe not every spirit, but try the spirits whether they are of God: because many false prophets are gone out into the world" (4:1). We are urged by John to "try" the spirits. We are urged not to be naïve enough to accept everything we hear in church as gospel! Heresies and false teachings were plentiful then and continue today. Many dare to stand and declare that they have "a word form the Lord." Yet, we know that all belief systems are not God's truth. So, John encourages us to "try" the spirits. We can test them by seeing whether they meet the criteria of "whatsoever things are true, whatsoever things are honest, whatsoever things are just, whatsoever things are pure, whatsoever things are lovely, whatsoever things are of good report; if there be any virtue, and if there be any praise, think on these things" (Phil. 4:8).

Excellence, I am not ashamed of the Gospel. I want to be a living testimony!

2 JOHN
LIFE LESSONS

2 JOHN 1

Doolittle is a character from the play Pygmalion (later, the movie My Fair Lady), who happens to embody the spirit of Second John's message. Professor Henry Higgins, a major word craftsman who came into her life, spun tales with his expansive vocabulary. In trying to work his magic of articulation upon this lady, she gets tired of his many empty words. Finally, in a huff she tells him, "Words, words! I'm sick of words. If you love me, prove it!" The apostle John had experienced true love in Jesus Christ. He knew love's virtues and manner of behaving. Jesus was the embodiment of love in truth and self-giving. So, as John remembers his Teacher and Friend, he writes to encourage the church to be like Jesus; to imitate His life and to follow His leadership in truthful love. "And this is love, that we walk after his commandments. This is the commandment, That as ye have heard from the beginning, ye should walk in it" (v. 6).

Lover of the Loveless, work in me that Your divine image is reflected in my deeds and not simply in my words.

3 JOHN
LIFE LESSONS

3 JOHN 1

Moving from issues of doctrine to the ethical matter of hospitality, John recalls the many individuals who had opened themselves, their homes, and their means to Jesus and the roving band of disciples for over three and one-half years. Without hospitality, their work would have been greatly impeded. So, hospitality was of primary concern as the mission ministry of the church. Gaius, a "wellbeloved" friend (v. 1), had been faithful in caring for the needs of visiting teachers sent by John (vv. 5–6). John's greeting is both a commendation and prayer for the one who lived out the mode of sharing love. "I wish above all things that thou mayest prosper and be in health, even as thy soul prospereth" (v. 2). Our spiritual and physical well-being are connected, for we are mind, body, and spirit. There is no separation of how we treat others and how that impacts us in various ways. "Diotrephes, who loveth to have the preeminence among them, receiveth us not.... neither doth he himself receive the brethren...Follow not that which is evil, but that which is good" (vv. 9–11).

A warm and gracious sign of welcome is a benchmark of the church of Jesus. Is it any wonder that in the average African-American church, the usher board is comprised of smiling sisters?

> ***Hospitable Host of Heaven,*** *thank You for flinging open the door to eternity and inviting me to come and be a welcome guest.*

JUDE LIFE LESSONS

JUDE 1

Jude, a servant of Jesus Christ and brother of James, a leader in the early church, writes to those who have been "sanctified," "preserved," and "called" by the life, words, and ministry of the Living Lord. He writes to encourage their faithful living of the doctrines and practices of the people of the Way. "It was needful for me to write unto you, and exhort you that ye should earnestly contend for the faith which was once delivered unto the saints" (v. 3). He prompts the church to return to the basics of salvation: trust in Jesus Christ.

> **Christ,** *My Solid Rock, help me to be firmly planted in the truth of Your Word.*

Apostasy means turning away form the truth of Christ and following "ways" that suit our individual fancy! False teachers had secretly "crept in unawares ... ungodly men, turning the grace of our God into lasciviousness, and denying the only Lord God, and our Lord Jesus Christ" (v. 4). The primary issue among the theologians of this period centered among the human-divine nature of Jesus. From this debate many concluded that what they believed far superseded how they lived and behaved. Ungodly living was practiced and encouraged. It was cheap grace at its best. Jude, however, warns: "These filthy dreamers defile the flesh, despise dominion, and speak evil of dignities.... Woe unto them!" (vv. 8, 11). These messages found listeners and practitioners! Jude calls the faithful to stand firm on truth. He also calls for the wayward to return to God's way of right living. "But ye, beloved, building up yourselves on your most holy faith, praying in the Holy Ghost.... Of some have compassion, making a difference: And others save with fear, pulling them out of the fire; hating even the garment spotted by the flesh" (vv. 20–23) Stand! Persevere! Hold on to your faith!

> **Lord,** *my prayer for all is this: "Unto him that is able to keep you from falling, and to present*

you faultless before the presence of his glory with exceeding joy, to the only wise God our Savior, be glory and majesty, dominion and power, both now and ever. Amen" (vv. 24–25).

REVELATIONS LIFE LESSONS

REVELATION 1

"The Revelation of Jesus Christ, which God gave unto him, to shew unto his servants things which must shortly come to pass" (1:1) This book is apocalyptic, meaning it reveals the mystery of Jesus Christ. It is a book of spectacular signs and symbols. It is a vision of the "end time" which Jesus allowed John to see and to share. In it the church is urged to hold and maintain high standards of right living. "Blessed is he that readeth, and they that hear the words of this prophecy, and keep those things which are written therein: for the time is at hand" (v. 3).

Jesus' identity as God is given: "I am t Alpha and Omega, the beginning and the ending, saith the Lord, which is, and which was, and which is to come, the Almighty" (1:8).

Almighty Coming Sovereign, I bow before You and cry with the host of angelic beings "Holy, holy,

holy, Lord God Almighty . . . Thou art worthy, O Lord, to receive glory and honour and power" (4:8, 11).

"I John, who also am your brother, and companion in tribulation, and in the kingdom and patience of Jesus Christ, was in the isle that is called Patmos, for the word of God, and for the testimony of Jesus Christ" (1:9). The church has always endured severe persecution for it stood against the social, political, economic, and religious norms of the day. Being a Christian has never been easy. Jesus suffered. The apostles suffered. You and I will suffer because of our faith!

The Roman officials had exiled John to an island about 50 miles from Ephesus. He had refused the Roman mandate to cease preaching the Good News of Jesus Christ. The message of truth is not popular today. Many of us have been "banished" and "exiled."

Suffering Savior, *in my times of exile, stand by me!*

The seven golden lampstands represent the congregations in Ephesus, Smyrna, Pergamos, Thyatira, Sardis, Philadelphia, and Laodicea. They faced great difficulty. John sees a vision of someone, "like unto the Son of man" (1:13). Jesus is in their midst with wisdom (white hair), judgment (blazing eyes), the priestly garb of forgiveness (robe and golden sash), and power (sharp double-edged sword and the seven stars).

As the apostle John begins his intentional study, led by the risen Jesus, the truth of the heart's intentions of various church members are exposed. For some, this is not a very pretty picture as Jesus explains: "I know thy works, and thy labour, and thy patience . . . and hast borne, and hast patience, and for my name's sake hast laboured, and hast not fainted. Nevertheless I have somewhat against thee, because thou hast left thy first love" (2:2–4).

> *First Love, forgive me for straying from You. Draw me back to Your fold. I long to be faithful.*

REVELATION 2

Jesus' warnings continue: "Repent; or else I will come unto thee quickly, and will fight against them with the sword of my mouth" (2:16). That is a promise He plans to keep. Sexual immorality ran rampant through the congregation at Pergamos. Many false teachers encouraged loose living. As a result many folks followed their teachings! Jesus follows His a severe rebuke with a haunting plea: "He that hath an ear, let him hear what the Spirit saith unto the churches" (v. 17).

Then Jesus adds this rebuke: "Thou sufferest that woman Jezebel, which calleth herself a prophetess, to teach and to seduce my servants to commit fornication, and to eat things sacrificed unto idols. . . . I will kill her children with death; and all the churches shall know that I am he which searcheth the reins and hearts: and I will give unto every one of you according to your works. But unto you I say, and unto the rest . . . that which ye have already hold fast till I come" (vv. 20, 23–25). Jezebel symbolizes the pagan queen who worshiped Baal and killed God's prophets (1 Kin. 18; 19). She represents a consistent threat of evil that runs through the church. She refuses to repent and be subject unto Israel's God. Her offspring live on! Avoid allowing sexual immorality and idolatry to make themselves at home in you!

> ***Holy One,*** *purify me, in word and in deeds. Rule all of me.*

REVELATION 3

Jesus continues with a few words to the church in Sardis: "I know thy works, that thou hast a name that thou livest, and art dead. Be watchful, and strengthen the things which remain, that are ready to die: for I have not found thy works perfect before God" (3:1–2). Good looks don't measure up! The call is to return to basic Christian truths and live the talk!

> ***All Knowing One,*** *help me to live devoted to Your holy ways.*

Jesus moves on to the church in Philadelphia: "Thou hast little strength, and hast kept my word, and hast not denied my name. . . . Behold, I come quickly; hold that fast which thou hast" (3:8, 11). Here is a commendation to faithful living.

> ***Witness of My Life,*** *help me to hold on!*

One of the most familiar rebukes in the Revelation is the one Jesus addresses to the church in Laodicea: "I know thy works, that thou art neither cold nor hot: I would thou wert cold or hot. So then because thou art lukewarm, and neither cold nor hot, I will spue thee out of my mouth" (3:15–16). Here is the most serious rebuke against mediocrity and indifference! This congregation was rich with material things and complacent about Christ who implored, "Behold, I stand at the door, and knock: if any man hear my voice, and open the door, I will come in to him, and will sup with him, and he with me" (v. 20).

Holy Presence, I invite you into my life, again and again.

REVELATION 4–5

Chapters four and five are filled with glorious visions of the world to come. "After this I looked, and, behold, a door was opened in heaven: and the first voice which I heard was as it were of a trumpet talking with me; which said, Come up hither, and I will shew thee things which must be hereafter" (4:1–2). The Lamb of God, the Lion of the Tribe of Judah, stands strong as the 24 elders and angelic host sing, "Worthy is the Lamb, that was slain to receive power, and riches, and wisdom, and strength, and honour, and glory, and blessing" (5:12).

Worthy Lamb, my heart, too, sings, "Amen!"

REVELATION 7–12

The revelation continues with a view of the saints in heaven—those who come through the tribulation. "After this I beheld, and lo, a great multitude, which no man could number, of all nations, and kindreds, and people, and tongues... And one of the elders answered, saying unto me, What are these which are arrayed in white robes? and whence came they?... And he said to me, These are they which came out of great tribulation, and have washed their robes, and made them white in the blood of the Lamb" (7:9, 13–14). The people of God come from everywhere. They all come through suffering! "They overcame him by the blood of the Lamb, and by the word of their testimony" (12:11). They all have been washed in the redeeming blood of Jesus Christ. And they have shared their testimony with others. There are two great aspects of our Christian faith that will be recognized through eternity. One is the matchless, redemptive blood of Jesus that has washed away our sin. The second is the record of our life in both word and deeds, which is recorded in the Lamb's Book of Life.

> ***Testimony of truth,*** *I realize that my life is a testimony of our relationship. Help me leave a worthy record of my love for You!*

"And there appeared a great wonder in heaven; a woman clothed with the sun, and the moon under her feet, and upon her head a crown of twelve stars: And she being with child cried, travailing in birth, and pained to be delivered....

The woman fled into the wilderness, where she hath a place prepared of God, that they should feed her there a thousand and two hundred and threescore days" (12:1, 2 6). John observes a great conflict in the heavens as an enormous red dragon with seven heads, seven horns, and seven crowns on his heads (v. 3) seeks to destroy the child of this pregnant woman. The dragon represents Satan, the evil one who is the power and authority of the kingdoms of this world. The woman represents the people who faithfully waited for the Deliverer, the Messiah. The child she carries is the Messiah.

"She brought forth a man child, who was to rule all nations with a rod of iron: and her child was caught up unto God, and to his throne" (v. 5). As Satan waits to devour the Child of the woman, God has prepared a place for her to be hidden for three and one-half years. This number might stand for the time between Jesus' first and second comings. It might also mean a period of time after the rapture of the church. "The woman were given two wings of a great eagle, that she might fly into the wilderness, into her place" (v. 14).

> ***Overcoming God,*** *You provide protection for me from the enemies' plans. You keep me safe from harm. Thank You!*

REVELATION 13

It is no secret that we are involved in a war. Satan hates God and God's people. Satan has followers and authority in this world. Satan knows his destiny and realizes that his time is drawing to a close. Satan understands that he is a defeated foe. "And he opened his mouth in blasphemy against God, to blaspheme his name, and his tabernacle, and them that dwell in heaven. And it was given unto him to make war with the saints, and to overcome them: and power was given him over all kindreds, and tongues, and nations. And all that dwell upon the earth shall worship him, whose names are not written in the book of life of the Lamb slain from the foundation of the world" (13:6–8).

> *Holder of the Book,* I told Jesus it would be all right to put my name in the Lamb's Book of Life. Daily, I'm checking on my name's registration!

REVELATION 17–19

One of the angels of the seven vials shows John another woman. "Come hither; I will shew unto thee the judgment of the great whore that sitteth upon many waters: With whom the kings of the earth have committed fornication, and the inhabitants of the earth have been made drunk with the wine of her fornication. . . . And upon her forehead was a name written, MYSTERY, BABYLON THE GREAT, THE MOTHER OF HARLOTS AND ABOMINATIONS OF THE EARTH. And I saw the woman was drunk with the blood of the saints, the blood of the martyrs of Jesus" (17:1–2, 5–6). This woman represents the evil "systems" of the world which have oppressed and slain the people of God. The Roman Empire is one that fits the description with its seven emperors. John the Revelator announces the fall of every evil system and the Lamb's seizing the final victory. "And the ten horns which thou sawest upon the beast, these shall hate the whore, and shall make her desolate and naked, and shall eat her flesh, and burn her with fire" (v. 16). As vengeance is enacted upon Babylon, and other sound is heard, that of "the voice of a great multitude, and as the voice of many waters, and as the voice of many thunderings, saying, Alleluia: for the Lord God omnipotent reigneth" (19:6).

> ***Reigning Monarch,*** *I want to sing in the heavenly choir. Attune my heart now to shout forth Your worthy praise.*

REVELATION 20–21

"And the devil that deceived them was cast into the lake of fire and brimstone, where the beast and the false prophet are, and shall be tormented day and night for ever and ever. . . . And whosoever was not found written in the book of life was cast into the lake of fire" (20:10, 15). This is the place of eternal punishment for all who do not place their faith in Jesus Christ. There are many different signs and symbols throughout this book. It required an in-depth study of both the prophecies found in Daniel and Ezekiel to begin a full overview of the complexity of these interwoven visions. What we need to remember is that every vision and symbol points us to the final victory of Jesus Christ and the peace that victory renders. John's closing image is of heaven—the final destination for all believers. "And I saw a new heaven and a new earth: for the first heaven and the first earth were passed away; and there was no more sea. And I John saw the holy city, new Jerusalem, coming down from God out of heaven, prepared as a bride adorned for her husband" (21:1–2).

> *Great God of Heaven and Earth, Oh, I want to be there with You, to be part of this happy day! Thank You for "The End" of the story. Thank You for salvation. Thank You for hope!*

REVELATION 22

The last words in Revelation point us to the glorious hope of Jesus' return. "I Jesus have sent mine angel to testify unto you these things in the churches. I am the root and the offspring of David, and the bright and morning star. And the Spirit and the bride say, Come.... He which testifieth these things saith, Surely I come quickly. Amen. Even so, come, Lord Jesus. The grace of our Lord Jesus Christ be with you all. Amen" (22:16–17a, 20–21).

> *Jesus, I echo John's words, "Even so, come, Lord Jesus!" (v. 21).*